WHAT IF?

*A running journey
from failure to first place*

Ashley Varley

Copyright © Ashley Varley 2024
This book is sold subject to the condition that it shall not, by way of trade or otherwise, be lent, resold, hired out, or otherwise circulated without the publisher's prior consent in any form of binding or cover other than that in which it is published and without a similar condition including this condition being imposed on the subsequent publisher.
The moral right of Ashley Varley has been asserted.
ISBN: 9798320395500

For Ernie and June.

Thank you for all your love and hugs.

CONTENTS

PREFACE 1
CHAPTER 1 LONDON MARATHON, APRIL 2016 3
CHAPTER 2 EVERYBODY HAS TO START SOMEWHERE 7
CHAPTER 3 ABINGDON MARATHON, OCTOBER 2016 16
CHAPTER 4 VIRGIN LONDON MARATHON, APRIL 2017 19
CHAPTER 5 LONDON TO BRIGHTON 100KM CHALLENGE,
MAY 2017 23
CHAPTER 6 RICHMOND MARATHON, SEPTEMBER 2017 31
CHAPTER 7 BRIGHTON 10KM, NOVEMBER 2017 35
CHAPTER 8 BRIGHTON MARATHON, APRIL 2018 38
CHAPTER 9 TRAINING 46
CHAPTER 10 THE ULTRAMARATHON DOUBLEHEADER, 2018 .. 52
CHAPTER 11 SOUTH DOWNS WAY 50, APRIL 2019 63
CHAPTER 12 LONDON MARATHON, APRIL 2019 70
CHAPTER 13 SOUTH DOWNS WAY 100, JUNE 2019 76
CHAPTER 14 HASTINGS PARKRUN, NEW YEAR'S DAY, 2020 88
CHAPTER 15 NORTH DOWNS WAY 100, AUGUST 2020 105
CHAPTER 16 LONDON MARATHON OCTOBER 2020 122
CHAPTER 17 THE END? 130
CHAPTER 18 NEW BEGINNINGS 134
CHAPTER 19 GOING UP! 140
CHAPTER 20 THAMES PATH 100 144
CHAPTER 21 STILL HIGHER! 149
CHAPTER 22 THE CCC 155
CHAPTER 23 ONE LAST DANCE 166
CHAPTER 24 FINAL THOUGHTS 180
CHAPTER 25 ERNIE AND JUNE 184
ACKNOWLEDGEMENTS 187

PREFACE

So, why write a book now? I've never achieved anything of note, and outside of my family and friends, my name would be unknown. You won't find me on Strava, and I don't have a large social media presence. Well, firstly, I'm currently nursing a slight calf strain, and when I'm bored, I eat! Therefore, if my fingers are tapping away at a keyboard, they aren't wrapping themselves around the lid of the biscuit tin. So, I guess it's a way of controlling my terrible eating habits! But there is another reason.

I'm a very ordinary runner, and my personal bests won't see me enter any record books. So, I ask myself once again, why write a book now? To be honest, it feels a little narcissistic to be doing this, and my reasons are a tad selfish. But by the end of my story, I hope it'll all make sense. I'm about to embark on my toughest running challenge yet, and my hope is that writing this book will keep me motivated during the hard winter training that lies ahead of me. Whether it's the thought of getting older or the knowledge that my fitness and speed might have begun to fade. Or could it be the understanding that one day, in the not-too-distant future, being the runner I aspire to be might not be achievable? Or even a combination of all the above - who knows! But something has made me consider the many miles I've covered. Over the years, I've completed numerous races, have lots of happy (and not so happy!) race memories and countless medals. These are supplemented by copious amounts of photographs of me looking fatigued and knackered. Taken by photographers who, very unfairly, took my picture when I wasn't looking at my best! One thing that's recently dawned on me though is I've no written record of my running (save for the odd social media posting). To date, I haven't put in writing how I felt during the build-up to a marathon or a new running goal or indeed, my experiences during a race or my thoughts and feelings in the immediate aftermath of a run. So, as I embark on a year that will see me take on the Centurion Running, one hundred-mile Grand Slam (4 x 100-mile races in six months), I thought it's about time I put pen to paper (or finger to keyboard) and made a record of my journey over the next twelve months. Having arrived at this decision, I then found myself thinking, I've been on quite a running voyage during the previous five years. A story of triumph and failure, of success and heartbreak, and redemption and discovery. All the while striving to be better and often thinking that was impossible and that I'd never reach the goals I dreamed of. So, why not write down my racing memories from those years too. It might be a good read; it might be rubbish. But just like with training to run a faster personal best, unless I try, I'll never know. This book will be part memoir covering the preceding four years of my running life, and part real-time journal following my attempts to prepare for and hopefully complete my four one hundred-mile races in six months. I invite you to join me on this voyage of memory and discovery, and we'll see where we end up! So, sit back, relax, and tag along as I take on the challenge of umpteen racing miles and thousands of training miles while consuming more energy drinks and gels than I thought was humanly possible! Let's begin.

CHAPTER 1

LONDON MARATHON, APRIL 2016

I love the London Marathon; in fact, I absolutely love it. It's definitely one of those races that I look forward to running the most. Without a doubt, it's up there with some of my favourite races. The famous landmarks that you pass on the route and the sights and sounds that one encounters during the marathon make for a sensory overload, and I, for one, adore soaking up every moment of it. The spectators and the volunteers are always loud and enthusiastic, and for me, they are a large part of what makes this event so special. I never tire of hearing the roars and the cheers and the endless encouragement that is offered to all of us runners. My wife (Jane) and I always travel to London on the morning of the race and find somewhere to park near Blackheath railway station. Normally, as we arrive, the "road closed" and "diversion" signs are beginning to be placed around the streets of Blackheath, and my fellow London Marathoners are starting to emerge from the railway station. Men and women of all ages, shapes, and sizes. Some look excited at the prospect of what is about to come, and some are clearly so nervous they look like they could throw up at any moment! The walk to the start is always a joy, and as you emerge onto Greenwich Park, the coloured blimps that identify each of the three start zones begin to loom large into view. They, alongside the many hot air balloons, looking resplendent, located adjacent to the red start, dominate the vista, making for an awe-inspiring sight. The sheer scale of the event is in evidence, taking my breath away, and the anticipation of the day ahead really starts to build. It's race day, and I can't wait!

Training leading up to the 2016 London Marathon has been somewhat sporadic, to say the least. And, if I'm honest, it's probably fair to say that I'm a little overweight – actually, I'm about two stone overweight! During 2015 and into the early part of 2016, Jane and I have been busy renovating our home, and that's led to all of the shenanigans that often accompany home improvements. We've probably all been there at one time or another. You know the sort of thing, numerous hours spent organizing various builders and suppliers and generally having your house turned upside down, while trying to live in the corner of one room, eating microwave meals! This, in turn, has led to not enough running on my part. This is a disgraceful excuse, of course. There is always time to run – at some point during the day - and I'd let the excuse of the inconvenience and upheaval of building work become a reason not to train. But it'll be fine; I've been running for years now, and in 2014, I ran the Brighton Marathon in 3:11:40. Ok, I wasn't quite as heavy as I am now (nowhere near in fact, but whatever!). But I've convinced myself that experience counts for so much, and by this point, I'd run plenty of marathons. This will easily make up for any lack of training miles. I could do this in my sleep! I'll take the conservative approach, see if I can find the 3:15 pacer, start with him, and then push on in the second half of the race. Sub 3 hours, ten minutes is mine today! Feeling suitably confident and ready, I make my way towards the starting pens, raring to go!

The weather is slightly overcast and not too hot – ideal for running, in fact, and as the start approaches, I spy the 3:15 pacer not far ahead of me. He's my target, and my first job of the day is to catch up with him. With thousands of runners crammed into such a small area, this is easier said than done! But after a few miles of bashing and barging my way past fellow runners, I find myself part of the sub 3:15 group. Now, I don't know if you've ever tried to stay with a pacer at a big city marathon, but it turns out that it isn't so easy. These guys are incredible runners, and their pacing is metronomic. They don't take any prisoners, and to stay on pace, he or she keeps passing slower runners in whatever way it takes. When you've got a dirty great flag on your back with numbers displaying your goal time, people seem more than happy to let you through, but they aren't always quite so accommodating for the guys and girls who are trying to stay with said pace group! Of course, I can't blame them – they have their own races to run – but it does mean that I find myself dodging from side to side and working hard just to stay with the pacemaker. Too hard, in fact, and I find myself wondering if I'll pay the price for this overexertion in the latter stages of the race. But for now, I'm revelling in the amazing London Marathon experience.

During the early stages, things are going well, and I'm feeling absolutely fine and full of confidence. By the time we approach halfway, I feel very much in control of my race, and I'm already starting to think about a new personal best. However, things begin to unravel quite worryingly by the time we'd reached mile eighteen. I'm beginning to breathe more heavily now – sucking in as much air as possible, and between miles twenty and twenty-one, things really start to fall apart! I'm now struggling to keep up with the pacer, and slowly, but surely, I'm beginning to drop back. This is seriously demoralizing, and the lack of training and poor physical shape that I'm in really start to take their toll. The wheels are about to fall off, and I'm powerless to prevent it. As I watch the 3:15 pace group slowly disappear into the distance, my run – that had now become a shuffle – turns into a walk. My race is run, and any chance of that new PB that I'd naively thought possible was gone. Somewhere between miles 19 and 20, a friend of mine caught up with me, and as she passes yours truly, she tries desperately to encourage me to keep going. But I had nothing left, and try as I might, I couldn't respond to her shouts of "COME ON ASH, KEEP GOING!". The highlight of the remainder of my race was spotting Jane at the 24-mile mark and getting a much-needed hug from my beautiful wife. I walked and jogged my way to the finish, crossing the line in 3 hours, 24 minutes, and 16 seconds.

I can't really say that I was disappointed with the run. This is the London Marathon, after all, and there are many runners who would give anything to be in my position. But I was disappointed with my own performance. This was a bit of a wake-up call, and the race showed that I'd reached a stage in my running life where on minimal training, I was no longer able to rock up on the day and run a time that I'd be satisfied with. If I wanted to get the best out of myself, then I was going to have to work hard for it.

In the days that followed the London Marathon, I found myself standing at a metaphorical fork in the road, contemplating my running. Sure, I'd been doing it for some time now, and I had some race results and running achievements that I was proud of. But what if I really tried? What if I got myself back in shape, got down to some hard work and proper training – I wonder if I could achieve even more? And so began a journey that would take me higher and further than I'd ever been before. Over trail, road, and mountain, witnessing breathtaking scenery, discovering more about myself along the way than I'd known before. The question of "What if?" was about to be answered.

CHAPTER 2

EVERYBODY HAS TO START SOMEWHERE

(A brief history of many running miles)

For me, running entered my life in the sort of way that I'm certain has a familiar ring to it for many people. During 1999, I was working for a utility company, and one member of our small team was a keen runner and had been for some years (he still is to this day). I can't quite remember exactly how it all came about, but during a conversation, the subject of our local Hastings half marathon came up. My colleague was a veteran of the race, and some bright spark had the idea of the four members of our team running the Hastings half marathon for charity. We had the dazzling brainwave of raising money for the children's ward at our local hospital. I couldn't quite comprehend what was happening, but, following a casual conversation over coffee, I was now facing the very real and frightening prospect of taking part in a half marathon! Initially, I'd been nervous and slightly daunted by the thought of running 13.1 miles, but I was only 27 years old, and it wasn't that long ago I'd been playing cricket and rugby on a regular basis. With a few weeks of training, I was convinced I'd be fine. This was early January, and I had until late March to get ready. In my tiny mind, that was ample time to prepare and turn myself into a runner. I went home that evening, feeling invigorated and ready to start my journey towards becoming a proper athlete. What could be easier!?

My first run didn't quite go to plan! I left my house wearing the only clothes that I possessed which kind of resembled running attire. This consisted of a pair of heavy cotton checked beach shorts – the sort of shorts that have one of those thin ropes sewn into them that you tie around your waist, and a loose-fitting, cotton T-shirt. My trainers were just trainers that I'd purchased because I thought they made some sort of fashion statement, and my socks were the same pair that I'd worn to work that day. I settled on a 1.5-mile lap that started and finished at my home, and as I closed the front door behind me, I was confident I'd return fairly quickly without too much damage to my lungs and legs. About ½ a mile into the run, my initial confidence had been somewhat dented, to say the least. I'd stopped twice and was already feeling like I wanted to throw up! What was this all about? This wasn't supposed to happen – surely, I was fitter than this. I walked, jogged, stumbled, and spluttered my way around the 1.5-mile circuit, and was extremely glad to make it back to the sanctity of my home in one piece, and still alive! It was at that moment the inevitable dawned on me. I had a lot of work to do over the coming weeks and months; this was going to be a much tougher challenge than I'd expected. I was seriously up against it and didn't I know it!

Over the next few weeks, I started to train every other night (still in my casual beachwear turned running attire), and slowly but surely, things began to improve. My confidence was given a real boost the night I ran with the rest of the team for the first time. They were fairly fit guys, and the prospect of running with them was a little disconcerting and nerve-wracking. I'd been running for about five weeks, and I guess it was time to see how my training was progressing. I was pleasantly surprised to find that not only did I manage to complete seven miles for the first time, but I didn't get left behind either. Feeling suitably satisfied, I thought to myself, "Maybe, just maybe, finishing this thing might be possible." Training continued over the next couple of months, and before I knew it, race day had arrived. Feeling sick, nervous, excited, and out of my depth, I made my way to the start, thinking I'll be glad when this is all over, and life can return to blissful normality again!

For the uninitiated among you, the Hastings half marathon is a tough race! Hastings is a hilly town, and the route of our half marathon has an elevation gain of nearly 1000ft (300m), with the majority of that ascent coming in the first five miles. It's a route that needs to be treated with respect, and going off too fast in the first five miles is at your peril. Guess who went off too fast in the first five miles!? I wouldn't know the full effects of my beginner's error until nearing the halfway mark when exhaustion suddenly took over. I was knackered and a long way from home. My glorious plan to run the whole thing had been thwarted, and now I was walking. I had been guilty of the classic beginner's mistake that, in the coming years, yours truly would advise many budding new runners not to make. I knew, first-hand, the cost of setting off too quickly. Struggling around the second half of the race was demoralizing and hard work, and I was relieved to finally reach the finish in a smidge under two hours. Overall, I was pleased with my achievement, but not how I'd gone about it! My first half marathon was done, and I was immensely proud to receive my finisher's horse brass. Making my way home, feeling happy and pleased, I thought, "I actually enjoyed that. Maybe I'll give it another go one day."

Throughout the next six years, this familiar pattern was played out on a yearly basis, and that was how running started to become a firm fixture in my life. At the turn of the year, I'd begin training, gain some fitness and run the Hastings half marathon. Over the years I got better and quicker and really looked forward to my annual jaunt around Hastings Town with much excitement and anticipation. To this day, I love this race. The route is challenging but fast if you pace it correctly – and of course, if the weather is on your side (the final 2.5 miles are run along the seafront promenade, and if you are unlucky enough to be confronted with a headwind, it's brutal, ruining many a potential PB). But most of all, in my opinion, the race is made by the spectators. With the exception of the big city marathons, I've never known so many people turn out to offer their support at a race. They cheer, clap, offer copious amounts of oranges and jelly babies to all and sundry, and wave homemade banners bearing words of support. Every year, there are bands and choirs dotted around the route, and it's the people of Hastings who are the real heroes of this race. They make the half marathon the event that it is, and after many years, it's no surprise that it continues to go from strength to strength. Long may it continue.

Around 2006, I decided that I might like to take my running a little further than my yearly racing ritual at the Hastings half, and for the first time in a calendar year, I found myself running beyond the end of March. Initially, I'd run on my own and then at some point during 2006 – encouraged by a friend – I joined a training night at a local running club. This proved to be a huge turning point in my running life, and it's where my love for this sport truly began to take hold. And what a perfect place the Hastings Runners Club was for me to develop and grow as a runner. Everyone welcomed me with open arms, making me feel at home from the start. Initially, I'd been sceptical about enlisting at a running club, feeling that I'd be out of my depth amongst proper runners, but that was certainly not the case. I was encouraged and supported at all times by such a great bunch of people, making friends that I still have to this day. What impressed me most about the club was that no matter what your level of ability, your goals, or reasons for running were, every member was of equal importance. That's such a noble and worthwhile quality for a club to have and should be an aspiration for any running group, because a running club should be open to runners of all abilities and goals. Over the next few years, running with the club became a three-day-a-week habit, punctuated by many races, ranging from 5km to the marathon distance, and my race performances steadily improved. I was loving running, and it had become a firm fixture in my life.

If I had to pick a favourite highlight from my earlier races, it would be the Hastings Marathon 2008. It was a one-off race, arranged to coincide with the centenary of the first marathon held in Hastings in 1908. The 2008 route would - as closely as possible - follow the same route as the original Edwardian race. It was an undulating and challenging run, embraced and well-supported by the folk of Hastings and the surrounding towns and villages. The race was organised by the Hastings Lions (the same team behind the successful Hastings half marathon), and they staged a memorable event. The reason this race stands out for me is that I got to run the whole thing with my great friend, Danny. Running alongside one another, we had an epic day out, encouraging and cajoling each other as we made our way around roads that we knew so well. We were brothers in arms united on an unforgettable day. What started out as a friendly, running rivalry between Dan and me developed into a firm friendship. To this day, we run together and can often be overheard discussing family life, kids, football, rugby, getting older – and anything else in between while we pound along our local streets and trails. Being able to share this incredibly special, one-off race with Dan is a memory I will always treasure.

I first started using running as a way of supporting charitable causes in 2008 at the London Marathon, and things quickly began to escalate from there. At first, raising money for charity occurred once a year at the London Marathon, and over the years, I raised funds for a number of charities. This continued until I began to expand my ideas and ambitions and started to arrange and organize my own charity challenges. These included Thomas' Challenge in 2013 and 6in6, in 2014.

Thomas' Challenge was set up in memory of a friend's son to raise money for a hospice that had supported the little man's family during some incredibly difficult and emotional times. Thomas was a brave boy with a ready smile. He has been a motivator and driving force for me, leaving a profound and lasting impact on my life. The challenge involved running 80 miles and cycling 50 over a three-day period. As well as other daft things like cycling on a stationary bike for 6 hours, outside a local Asda superstore. Trust me, my backside was numb after 6 hours in the saddle! Thomas' Challenge was the toughest thing I'd ever done to date, but with the help of some friends who joined me on the way, somehow, I made it to the end.

In Spring 2014, a running friend approached me and asked if I could help raise funds for a little boy who lived in our hometown. The young lad had been born with a rare illness that essentially meant the nerves sending signals to his legs were not wired correctly, leaving him unable to walk for anything other than a short distance. Even then, he needed the aid of a frame to help him get about, and he was forced to spend lots of time in a wheelchair. His parents were trying to raise funds to pay for pioneering surgery, only available in the USA. If successful, this surgery would give their son a chance to walk and potentially run without any aids. I came up with the plan of pushing the lad around the Hastings Half marathon in his wheelchair, in an effort to raise funds for his cause. When I approached his parents, they were understandably sceptical; I mean, who wouldn't be? But, after a few runs with their son, a friendship and trust blossomed, and we found a way of making it work in which the young man would be safe and happy. So it was that at the end of March, we ran around the Hastings half marathon route – hills and all! I remember thinking, as we lined up at the start amongst thousands of runners, a heavy weight of responsibility on my shoulders. It was my job to look after my little friend and get him safety around the thirteen-mile route! Why had that only just dawned on me!? Once underway, my nerves disappeared, and we had an awesome and memorable run. Approaching the finish, zigzagging from side to side, we lapped up the applause and adulation dished out by the many spectators lining the road to the finish. My new pal was enthusiastically squeezing the rubber ball on the end of his old school, brass horn that my wife had given him. Announcing our arrival at the finish with a toot-toot! Many people in Hastings really embraced our run and offered generous donations to the cause. I'm proud to have played a small part in the journey of this family, and it's immensely pleasing to be able to report the surgery was a success. There were still weeks and months of physiotherapy and hard work ahead for the brave boy, but nine years on, and now a teenager, he continues to go from strength to strength.

In Autumn 2014, 6in6 was born as a way of supporting the Lewis Moody Foundation. Former Leicester Tigers, Bath, and England Rugby World Cup-winning legend, Lewis Moody, established his charity in memory of a fifteen-year-old boy that he'd come to know well. Sadly, the boy in question passed away less than a year after their first meeting. I'm a huge rugby fan, and Jane and I were due to attend the opening fixture of the new Premiership rugby season, known as the London Double Header. The fixture involved two matches, played by the four Premiership teams based in and around London at the time, and the matches were to take place at Twickenham stadium. As Jane and I were going anyway, I had the bright idea of running to Twickenham. It would require me to run six marathons, in six days, hence the unquestionably brilliant and original name 6in6! In principle, the concept was great, but the organization was a nightmare! The trouble was that I'd approached Lewis with my proposal long before we'd entered the planning stage. Lewis loved the idea, and suddenly, Jane and I were tasked with arranging the whole thing. This resulted in endless hours spent plotting the course, and if my memory serves me well, we ended up driving the entire route 4 times! The strategy was that Jane would be in the car while I ran from my home in Hastings to Twickenham stadium, and we'd stop off at all four rugby clubs that were involved in the games.

Much to our surprise – it worked! Jane was my support crew, carrying everything that I needed, and she would leapfrog me as I ran, servicing my needs – so to speak! We stayed in cheap hotels at the end of each day, and the route took us from Hastings to Wadhurst, on to Tunbridge Wells, Sunbury-on-Thames (where the training ground of London Irish RFC was located), Adams Park, Wycombe (where Wasps RFC played their home games at the time), Allianz Park, Hendon, London (home of Saracens RFC), and finally, Twickenham, where the mighty Harlequins FC are based a stone's throw from the home of England rugby – Twickenham stadium. Looking back now, it was mad, but it was so much fun! When we arrived at Twickenham stadium, Lewis Moody was there to greet us. Standing about 18 inches taller than me, he gave me a huge hug, nearly crushing my ribs! As part of Lewis' duties that day, he was working with vehicle manufacturer, Land Rover. As a treat, fortunate Land Rover owners could have their photos taken with Lewis, alongside the William Webb Ellis Trophy – more simply known as the trophy awarded to the winners of the Rugby World Cup. Suddenly, I heard a voice say to me, "Ash, would you like to have your photo taken with me alongside the trophy?" That voice belonged to Lewis, and I didn't need to be asked twice! I took my place on one side of the trophy, with Lewis on the other, and then he inquired, from a lady standing nearby, "Have you got the white glove?" She came over with said glove and handed it to me. Lewis told me to slip it on and said that we could hold the William Webb Ellis Cup together! What a moment this was! With a gloved hand, I picked up one side of the trophy, while Lewis held the other, with his bare hand. While our photograph was being taken, Lewis turned to me and asked, "Do you know why you are wearing the glove?" "No," was my reply. "Because unless you were part of a team that won it, you can never touch it with your bare hands." I remember thinking, "Oh, wow!" As if this moment wasn't special enough, it'd now been elevated into a whole new stratosphere! Here I am, stood next to this legend of rugby union. A man who literally felled opponents for England and made more than his fair share of tackles for his teammates, and I'm holding the greatest prize that rugby union has to offer with him. The glove that I was wearing represented an appropriate and apt barrier between me and a trophy that I'd played no part in winning. This is a moment that I'll treasure for my lifetime, and the photo captured on that day, bearing Lewis' signature, hangs proudly in my home.

My various charity challenges have – so far – raised around £16,000, and I'm enormously proud of that. When we talk about running, we often talk about our personal bests. These charity ventures that I've enjoyed participating in represent the best that I can be. I'm lucky that when I said to some poor, unsuspecting soul "I've had a brilliant idea" many of them put their trust and belief in me and came along for the ride! Together, we did some wonderful things, raising funds for deserving causes along the way.

I couldn't possibly end this brief resume of my running life without talking about the greatest prize that this magnificent sport has afforded me. I first met Jane while marshalling at a 5km, club race in 2013. We got talking and hit it off immediately. To cut a long story short, I proposed to Jane in 2017, and in 2018, she did me the honour of becoming my wife. We've been on some amazing adventures together, and Jane is my greatest supporter, offering endless encouragement in whatever I do. Jane brings love and happiness into my world in a way that I could never have imagined possible. She's a constant source of light in my life, and I love her dearly. Thank you, running, for bringing us together and providing me with my wonderful wife!

CHAPTER 3

ABINGDON MARATHON, OCTOBER 2016

In the aftermath of the unmitigated failure that was the 2016 Virgin London Marathon, several thoughts were whizzing around my mind. It's all very well to have the grand idea of trying to be the runner I thought I could be, but it's a whole different thing to put it into practice. I'm 44 now, and not getting any younger. What if my best years are behind me? What if, despite my best intentions, I just don't have what it takes to improve anymore, to be a better runner? Yes, I'd been more committed to my training since the London Marathon than I had been for some years. I hope it's gone well; I think it's gone well, and I'm lighter than I was in April too. Can I really do this? As the Abingdon Marathon approached, the pre-race nerves were more heightened than ever before. This was going to be the first test of my much improved fitness, training, and race craft since London. Time to find out if all the hard work has paid off.

The Abingdon Marathon is another favourite race of mine. It's organised by a trio of running groups made up of the Abingdon Athletic Club, Headington Road Runners, and White Horse Harriers Athletics Club, and together they do a superb job of staging the event. The race starts and finishes at Tilsley Athletics track; it has a five-hour cut-off limit, and the course is fast and flat, giving competitors the chance of a fast run. There are many club vests on show and few fancy dress outfits, giving the event the feel of a proper race. This is a run where you go to give your all, and I love that.

Jane and I drove up to Oxfordshire on race morning and decided to take the latest addition to our family with us. He is a Chihuahua/Jack Russell cross, named Toby, and at the time, he was only 12 weeks old. He's small now but back then he was minute! I can promise you that this little bundle of excitement was the star of the show, and he made many new friends while we were there! Having Toby with us was fun and relaxing, and it helped to take my mind off the pre-race tension. After London had gone so wrong for me, my confidence and pride were a little dented, leading to innumerable pre-race nerves and negative thoughts. This was going to be a challenging run, and I knew it.

The weather was slightly overcast and dry as the race began. These conditions are perfect for me, and I quickly settled into a steady rhythm and took my spot in the pack. The plan was to run at a 3:10 pace, with consistent mile splits, but by the halfway point, it became obvious that I'd gone off a bit too quickly, and I was actually closer to running a 3:05. Knowing I wasn't capable of sustaining that sort of speed for the whole marathon, I took the prudent decision to ease back a little. The route itself consists of two laps that travel through the villages of Drayton, Milton, and Sutton Courtenay. I wouldn't describe the route as the most picturesque marathon in the world, but there are a couple of points where it passes by the River Thames, making for especially pretty views. Reaching the Thames for the second time, it became clear that my rush of adrenaline during the first half of the race was catching up with me. I was beginning to struggle, and my speed was dropping. However, a sub 3:10 might still be possible if I dug deep and kept battling through. With two miles to go, I was definitely entering the pain cave! Time to get my head down, grit my teeth, and keep going. Throughout the final couple of miles, my legs were like jelly, and I was at breaking point. Fighting cramp and aching like a struggling achy thing, in the end, I crossed the finish line in 3:09:47 – a new PB for me! Feeling shattered but delighted and pleased that the race had come to an end, a hug from Jane was the perfect post-race treat!

As we made our way home (with a very tired Toby), I was thrilled with my result. Ok, I'd been slowing towards the latter stages of the race, having messed up my pacing strategy. But this was a step in the right direction. It was a small step, yes, and my race plan needed a lot of work. But my confidence was on an upward curve. Time to recover and then start building towards my next challenge – the 2017 Virgin London Marathon.

CHAPTER 4

VIRGIN LONDON MARATHON, APRIL 2017

Preparations leading into the 2017 edition of the London Marathon had been extremely positive, and my running was in a good place. I'd decided to use one of the training plans developed by elite running coach Martin Yelling, available on the London Marathon website, as a training guide. I'd be following a structured marathon training plan that incorporated regular speed work for the first time. This proved to be a real step up in intensity for me, resulting in better, more consistent performances in my build-up races, not to mention a lot of hard work! In February, I ran the Tunbridge Wells half marathon in a time of 1:25:42, and then I crossed the finish line of the Lydd 20-mile race in March in 2:19:00. To say I was pleased with these results would be an understatement, and both proved to be a real boost to my confidence just in time for the London Marathon in April. This was a very positive move in the right direction.

Some of my friends were confidently telling me that this would be my sub-three-hour marathon year. But I knew in my heart I was far from ready for that. Executing my race strategy correctly and gaining a new PB were the only things on my mind, and as the big day arrived, that was all I was focusing on.

Before I knew it, race day was upon us, and Jane and I made our way up to London. We arrived in Blackheath and joined the human train that makes its way up the hill from the town centre to Greenwich Park. The first port of call for me is always the queue for the portaloos! (Top tip: it is a good idea to include a loo roll in your race bag – they often run out!) Feeling excited and nervous, all at the same time, I made my way into the green starting zone and handed my bag over to a friendly volunteer on the baggage lorries. I used the loo, one last time, said goodbye to Jane, and made my way to my starting pen. Saying goodbye to Jane is a bit of a ritual for me, signifying that things are about to get serious. I kiss her through the fencing dividing the runners from our loved ones and supporters, look her straight in the eye, and then, as I turn away, I start thinking to myself, this is it – time to go to work!

I can't stand the wait in the starting pens! I'm pumped up and ready now; I need to get running, and the closer it gets to start time, the longer the seconds and minutes seem to drag. By this stage, I've been building up to this moment for months and I want to get started! The sound of the gun going off, signalling the race is underway comes as a massive relief. Finally, after what feels like an age, the race is go!

I settled into my stride quickly and at about the 2-mile point, I passed one of the 3:15 pace groups. Running by, I glanced across and saw the group was being led by a gregarious and lovable chap whom I'd met before. On a couple of occasions in the past, I've been lucky enough to find myself paced by David. He always brings a wonderful sense of fun to his groups and is forever encouraging and happy. I shouted out, "Good morning, David," and he looked across at me replying, "F**k me! There is nothing of you!" Clearly, I was looking a little different since he last spotted a slightly cuddlier version of me at the 2016 London Marathon! "I'm aiming for 3:10 today," I shouted, and David wished me the best of luck and on I went. Reaching the amazing Cutty Sark and the equally amazing crowds around that part of the run, I was bang on pace and feeling great. Shortly after passing the beautiful ship, I came alongside one of the many aid stations on the route, and I was struggling to get close enough to grab one of the drinks from the tables. Luckily, an extremely nice chap saw me straining to reach over and kindly offered me the remainder of his bottle. Unbelievably, that chap turned out to be a good friend of mine. I'd trained with Paul during the build-up to the race, and seeing him was a real adrenaline boost. What are the chances of that happening among 40,000 runners? The miles drifted by as we chatted and soaked up the atmosphere. I can remember the awesome feeling of running across Tower Bridge with a good friend, listening to the cacophony of noise emanating from the crowd while thinking; this is just the greatest feeling ever! We continued to wind our merry way past the spectators and the bands, gently encouraging each other and chipping away at the miles through the Isle of Dogs and Canary Wharf. Approaching ¾ race distance, I was feeling good and full of energy. Paul must have noticed because he encouraged me to push on, and push on, I did. It was at this point my race truly came alive; I was pushing the pace and loving it! Feeling about 6ft tall (quite something for a short bloke like me!), I shoved my shoulders back, thrust my chest out, and with my head held high, I felt like I was running on air. At one point, I passed a spectator who shouted, "Ash, you've got this!" Damn right I have, I thought! 23 miles into a hard race, heads were dropping and running form was fading all around me while I was getting faster and faster. It sounds awful to me now, but I found myself thinking I'm the one who has got this nailed and I'm showing everyone how this should be done – look at me go! This is completely out of character for me, and if I passed you on that day, looking determined and focused, I'm sorry! I'd like to apologise to you unreservedly for being such a show-off! Continuing on in this manner along the embankment, the London Eye, Cleopatra's Needle, and Big Ben seemed to disappear in a blur. Not until, approaching St James Park (around the 25-mile point) did I start to tire. But I wasn't about to let up – not today. Turning onto The Mall, I headed for the finish, crossing the line in 3:05:02 – a massive new PB for me and a negative split to boot. It couldn't have played out any better. Bumping into Paul was a real stroke of luck. A veteran of a 3:02 marathon a few years previously, his experience proved invaluable. Both Paul and I were aiming for sub 3:10 finishes and working together, we made it past 20 miles bang on pace. Paul didn't quite make it under 3:10 on this occasion, but he played a huge part in my success. Far more significantly than that, it was a privilege to run this most brilliant of marathons in the company of a friend. Yet another wonderful memory made.

One of the statistics from that day that stands out for me is this one. Over the final 7.2k of the race, the London Marathon organisers recorded how many people you passed – or who passed you – during that passage of the race, and they shared that on your individual results page. On that day in April 2017, I passed 677 people over the final 7.2k, and no one passed me – not one single person. At long last, I'd got my race tactics spot on. Finally proving to myself that I could run a hard but controlled first half over the marathon distance and then accelerate progressively during the second half. In many ways, getting my race plan right mattered more to me than my finish time. A year of hard work and determination had paid dividends. My self-belief was sky-high, and I couldn't wait for the next race. I decided there and then to enter another marathon as quickly as I could.

CHAPTER 5

LONDON TO BRIGHTON 100KM CHALLENGE, MAY 2017

I had been contemplating the possibility of attempting an ultra-marathon since completing 6in6. That was a multi-day affair, involving running approximately a marathon a day for six days, but I wondered, could I run further than the marathon distance in one day? Over morning coffee, on a cold winter's day, I found myself discussing this very thought with Jane. I'm not sure what brought the subject into our conversation, maybe it was one of those social media adverts or something, but the upshot of our discussion was, I now found myself with a place in the 2017 London to Brighton Challenge. It sounds like a rash decision, I know, but I promise you, we did give it at least some thought!

The race is about 80% off-road, 100 kilometres (62 miles) in length and consists of towpaths, country lanes, beautiful woodland, and stunning downland trails. This challenge is part of a series that's organised by a company called Ultra Challenge, and there were a few reasons that we chose this particular event. Firstly, it finished in Brighton, meaning that I'd be running back towards my home from the very start. This, I figured, would act as a motivational tool if I began to flag during the latter stages. Secondly, the total elevation gain over the 62 miles is about 1500m, which isn't that tough when compared to some other ultras. And thirdly, Ultra Challenge organizes their challenges for both runners and walkers, resulting in the cut-off times at each aid station being eminently achievable. Because of the length of these races, participants are expected to arrive at each aid station along the route within a specified time. This is for safety and logistical reasons and is completely necessary. Because I'd be attempting to combine running with some walking, my aim was to be well inside the cut-off times. Well, that was the plan, anyway! I felt I'd need all the help I could get just to complete 62 miles on foot! Not having to think about cut-off times would ease some of the pressure I'd put myself under by simply entering the darn thing! Sometimes, I find myself wondering, "Why do I have these mad ideas!?"

Though this sort of distance was completely new to me, I hadn't really considered any specific training. My priority since January had been preparing for the London Marathon. The upshot of that being, I'd done little trail running and no real hill work in preparation for this race. But, in blissful ignorance of the challenge that lay ahead, I wasn't too concerned by that. My theory was, I'm fit, in good shape because of the marathon training that I've been doing, and I had 5 weeks between the marathon and this race to recover. The thought process behind my race strategy was, I'm confident I can comfortably complete a marathon, so if I slow my usual pace down, and take it steady, I should be able to complete just over double the marathon distance. Piece of cake, right?! And so, it was that, on an overcast May morning, Jane and I left our home for the drive to Richmond where the race would begin.

We arrived at the event headquarters to be welcomed by a sea of sponsors' flags, marquees, and coffee and food outlets. There was inspirational music being played loudly, and runners and walkers nervously pacing about, waiting for the start. Good, I thought, I'm not the only one with pre-race nerves! Participants had the option of starting their races anywhere between 6:30 am and 10 am. I'd decided to start at 9 am, believing that I'd hopefully be able to catch up with some of the walkers ahead of me throughout the first half of the race. That way, I wouldn't be alone for long, which I theorised would reduce my risk of missing one of the course markers and getting lost! As my allotted start time approached, my fellow participants and I were called into the start area for the obligatory warm-up! You know the sort of thing, where an overly enthusiastic and keen instructor stands on a stage with one of those microphones that wrap around their heads. He or she then goes through an energetic routine while barking out instructions to his/her audience. I'm completely uncoordinated, and I was rubbish and struggled to keep up. To be honest, my main concern was avoiding punching the person next to me in the face! Once all of the aerobic shenanigans were done, feeling particularly invigorated, I said goodbye to Jane, joined in with the 10-second countdown (with suitable gusto!) and then we were off!

The run route took us across Old Deer Park and very quickly onto the Thames towpath, passing beautiful barges and sailing boats along the way. The course continued, following the river before turning inland near Kingston-upon-Thames. Making my way along the scenic towpath, I passed some of the walkers who'd started ahead of me. While passing them, I relished calling out words of encouragement and support, and I wondered what was going through each of their minds as together, we tackled this mammoth task. My pre-race nerves had vanished by this point, and I was savouring the journey and the challenge ahead. 12k into the run, I arrived at the first aid station, and what a smorgasbord of delights awaited the hungry runner! Coming from a road racing background, I was used to aid stations consisting of water, maybe an energy drink or an energy gel, and if you were really lucky, a jelly baby or two. But this, this was a whole new world of delectable delights! There were crisps, biscuits, chocolate, bars, cakes, peanuts, coke, and squash and the requisite water, gels, and energy drinks. There was so much choice; one couldn't decide what to tuck into first! I thought to myself, I suspect it would be possible to consume more calories during the race than you could burn off while running the whole distance! As if that were not enough, there was tea and coffee and even chairs scattered around, so that a tired, beleaguered runner could put his/her feet up for a while and have a rest! I was loving this new ultra-running world that I'd entered!

Once I'd enjoyed my fill of goodies, it was time to get back to the task at hand. On a beautiful Spring day, the route continued through the town of Stoneleigh and the beautiful Nonsuch Park. Then onto Sutton before entering the second checkpoint at Oaks Park. By this stage, pleased with my progress, I was smiling from ear to ear. On we went through Coulsdon, and the stunning surroundings of Farthings Down, Devilsden Wood, and Happy Valley Park. Shortly after Happy Valley, the route takes you under the M25 motorway and at this juncture, I came across the very strange sight of a lady running in rather peculiar and unexpected footwear! She'd decided to make what was already quite a stern challenge, even harder, by running in her wellies! Can you believe that? Looking down at my comfy trainers, I felt slightly lacking! My legs were feeling fine, approaching the marathon distance at 40k in a little over 4 hours, though I was slightly concerned about the pace at which I'd been progressing. Had I gone off too fast yet again? It was somewhere between 45k and the halfway point at 56k that things started to get tougher. I was beginning to get a bit tired as midway approached, and the smile that had been beaming from ear to ear was now turning into a slightly concerned frown.

I was so pleased to reach the halfway aid station at Tulley's Farm just outside Turners Hill. I hadn't been drinking enough fluid and stupidly (again!), going way too fast. In desperate need of a rest, it was heartening to see Jane awaiting my arrival. A friend of mine had already reached the rest stop, and the poor chap was suffering knee trouble. He had decided that he was going to call it a day at this point because his knee was just too painful to carry on. I offered to walk the rest of the way with him, but his mind was made up. Finding a chair, I sat down in what is best described as an alfresco restaurant! If I'd thought the food selection at the previous aid stations had been impressive, this was something else! As well as the aforementioned assortment of goodies, there was also pasta, burgers, and chicken! Ignoring all of that, I headed straight for two slices of chocolate cake and a nice cup of tea to wash it down with! How very decadent! Honestly, you'd think I was out for a leisurely afternoon tea and cake rather than taking on a 100-kilometre race! After enjoying an unhurried break, Jane helped me into some fresh clothes, I had a chat with a few fellow runners, and then after about half an hour, it was time to leave the comfort of Tulley's Farm.

I decided that, because I'd been sat down for a while, it would be better to walk for a few minutes before attempting to run – just to loosen off my legs. That done, I tried to break into a jog. Immediately, my calf muscles began protesting and cramping, and the ensuing pain was excruciating. I walked for a while and then tried again and got the same result. After the third or fourth attempt, tentatively I got going – very slowly and extremely cautiously.

So here I am, tired, sporadically suffering from cramp and still with nearly half of the run to complete. Sitting down for so long had been a huge mistake and I was definitely paying the price for my foolishness. Not only that, but I was also starting to feel demoralised and defeated. It was at this point that it hit me… "So, this is what ultra-running is all about! This isn't just about going a bit further, while running a bit slower; this is much tougher than that. It's about discipline, commitment, learning to deal with adversity, mind over matter and sheer grit and determination." This was turning into a difficult lesson and if I were to make it to the end, I needed to learn very quickly.

From that point, I opted to take my time, jogging when I was able and walking when I needed to. Most important of all, I chose to stop seeing the race distance holistically. Instead, I'd break it up and try and get from aid station to aid station. If I could achieve these small victories, bit by bit, I might just make it to the end.

The next stop was Wivelsfield aid station, and passing the race timing beacon, I uttered to myself, "Yes, you've made it, Come On!" Instead of ludicrous amounts of cake, this time I chose a banana and salty crisps to help ward off the cramp and opted not to sit down! "Don't hang around here too long," I thought to myself, "you have to keep moving now." Trudging ever onwards, somewhere between 60km and 70km, my phone beeped, announcing a text message from my Dad that simply read: "You are doing amazing AD, keep going!" (The AD comes from my forename initials and my Dad is the only person is the world who refers to me by that acronym). Unbeknownst to me, he'd been following my progress on the Ultra Challenge website throughout the day. I'd not heard from anyone up to this point, and that message was just the boost I needed. My legs were sore, and I was exhausted, but Dad's text put a smile on my face and really helped to lift my mood. With my morale much improved, I pushed on towards aid station eight at Plumpton College.

Plumpton College is 88km into the race – just 12km to go! I popped into the rest stop and was enthusiastically greeted by the wonderful aid station staff. A fellow runner had informed me that there was a bit of a climb after Plumpton. I asked one of the volunteers if that was correct, and she looked at me with a knowing look and – like a concerned Mother said, "Yes dear, there is a bit of a hill!" Swallowing hard I took a packet of Hula Hoops and left the friendly volunteers behind me, full of dread as I thought about what was to materialize in front of me. How steep was this hill?

It turned out they weren't kidding when they said there was a bit of a hill! About 1km outside of Plumpton, there, stood in front of me, was a monstrous hill! With battered legs, and feeling knackered, this thing looked like Mount Olympus to me! Taking a deep breath, I tentatively headed on up. As climbing this mountain would involve a bit of walking, I decided to eat the crisps that I'd taken from the aid station. However, by this stage, I couldn't swallow! No matter how much I chewed, these bloody things refused to go down. Ultra-running was turning out to be a huge test in many unexpected ways. Eventually, I made it to the top of the hill and onto the beautiful South Downs. The chalk path laid out in front of me was rugged, but flat, so I decided to attempt a gentle jog. A couple of ladies came past me, and I resolved to try and stay with them if at all possible. Running along the top of the ridge, suddenly, like a beacon of hope, or a shining light in a dark tunnel, I saw on the horizon in front of me what can only be described as the beautiful sight of the Brighton Community Stadium! Looking majestic in the warm glow of a late Spring evening, with the sun glinting off its walls, this was an emotive sight, providing me with some much-needed impetus. If I could see the stadium, then we were near Falmer, meaning we were just outside of Brighton. "Come on Ash, you just have to keep putting one foot in front of the other." This was such a massive lift, and before I knew it, I'd crossed the bridge over the A27 (which bypasses Brighton), and I was on my way up the final hill towards Brighton. Only 4km to the end.

The race finish was located at Brighton racecourse, and cresting the hill in the little village of Woodingdean, I could see the racecourse grandstand. Dusk was beginning to settle, and it was getting dark. I couldn't cope with the thought of wrestling my headtorch out of my backpack, and so I pressed on a little faster. The final 1km was on the racecourse itself with the finish line, adjacent to the main grandstand, and I've never been so happy to see a finish line, looming into view! Despite all of the ups and downs, I was actually going to finish this thing! Since halfway, I wasn't sure that I'd make it. It'd taken everything I had to reach the end, and I was utterly exhausted! Approaching the finish gantry, I saw Jane who was shouting and cheering; I was overjoyed to see her. I finally crossed the line at 8:42 pm, eleven hours and forty-two minutes after I'd left Richmond. Shattered and broken, I found Jane, and she gave me a huge and satisfying hug. Though there was plenty of food on offer, I didn't want to eat. I just wanted to get in my car and go home to the comfort of my bed. My first Ultra was done. And though it had been a roller coaster ride, with many ups and downs in a strange and sadistic sort of way, despite aching all over, I thought to myself, "I enjoyed that!"

CHAPTER 6

RICHMOND MARATHON, SEPTEMBER 2017

The marathon I chose to follow up the success I'd experienced in London, came in the form of the Richmond marathon. Billed as the fastest marathon in the capital, it's flat as a pancake. The course travels from Kew Gardens before following the Thames towpath and crossing Kingston Bridge. It then continues to Hampton Court Palace and the turnaround point at 14 miles. From here, the route crosses Kingston Bridge once again before returning to the towpath and onto the finish in Old Deer Park. It certainly is a picturesque route, and the atmosphere in the race village is awesome!

I'd decided after the London Marathon that I was going to have a stab at breaking three hours over 26.2 miles for the first time. My confidence was high, and I felt ready to tackle what was personally for me, the Holy Grail of race results. Once again, I'd been following one of Martin Yelling's race plans, and I was happy with the way my training had gone.

So that we wouldn't have to rush around on the morning of the run, Jane and I decided to stay near Richmond the night before race day. This was supposed to be a relaxing way to head into the marathon. However, things didn't quite go to plan! We had a nightmare journey, and when we finally arrived at our hotel, it was late into the evening. I say hotel, but that is to give it a rather grand title! We'd decided to stay in a budget chain bed & breakfast (that shall remain nameless!) Our room was about the size of a shed, and there was no carpet, just plastic flooring throughout. I think that this type of accommodation might be referred to as a pod, and they are not particularly comfortable. But it was okay, and we slept reasonably well. More disconcerting was the cockroach that was climbing up the wall when we awoke in the morning. We showered in seconds, packed our stuff up in a flash, and we were out of there!

I felt good as I joined my fellow runners behind the start line waiting for the final few minutes to tick by before the race got underway. When it did, I quickly settled into the 6:52 minute miles that I'd require to finish the marathon in three hours. I'd be following a nutrition plan that involved taking advantage of the many drinks stations on the course and consuming one of the energy gels that I was carrying every five miles. Things were going great as I exited Old Deer Park and headed down the Thames towpath. If anything, my pace was a little too fast, but I figured that would give me some time in the bank approaching the latter stages of the race. Sticking to my nutrition plan, I passed Hampton Court Palace, around halfway, and ate my third gel. By this point, I was around 4 minutes ahead of a three-hour finish time and beginning to think, "This is it! I'm finally going to have a marathon time that starts with a 2!" It was around the 18-mile mark that things started to change dramatically.

Out of nowhere, I was starting to breathe heavily. I was labouring, and my running form had begun to slide. I could feel my shoulders dropping as I began leaning forward, as if reaching out, desperately, in a futile effort to go faster. The watch I was wearing had a function that monitored how far I was ahead of the 6:52 pace required to get under 3 hours. Approaching 19 miles, I was still about three minutes inside my target time. "You must keep running!" I exclaimed to myself. Shortly after this, fatigue and exhaustion meant that the urge to take a walking break became overwhelming. Slowing to a walk, and becoming increasingly desperate, I chose to eat the last two gels that I was carrying to try and give me a boost. I was now only 2 minutes ahead of race pace as I began running again. Only ½ a mile later, I'd stopped for a second time. Another short break, and now only 1 minute ahead of my requisite pace, I started running once more. By this stage, I was fully aware that if I stopped again, this would all be over, and I'd have failed miserably.

Desperately, I tried to keep going, but try as I might, I was powerless to stop the relentless decline. I checked my watch to find I was 40 seconds ahead of my required pace, then 30, then 20, and then finally – like a kick to the stomach – it happened. My eyes were rigidly fixed on my wrist as I went from 5 seconds ahead of my race pace to 5 seconds behind it. I'd hit the wall and there was nothing I could do about. I'd been desperate to break three hours and my dream was fading right there and then. Once again, my run turned into another walk, and, feeling dejected, I turned off my watch – I couldn't bear to look at it anymore. By this point, somewhere between 21 and 22 miles, I just wanted my race to end. To add insult to injury, nearing the 25-mile point, I was passed by the 3:10 pacer. That was enough for me, and I walked nearly all the way to the end, crestfallen, sad and demoralised. Finally arriving at the finish line, I saw my endlessly proud wife, clapping and cheering. My response to her, "I've had a bloody awful race!" I broke the timing beam in 3:18:59. I picked up my medal and stomped off to find Jane.

In the immediate aftermath of the race, I blamed just about anything and everything except myself for my failure. The course, the hotel we had stayed in, the journey up to Richmond the night before – in fact, just about any reason I could think of that didn't involve yours truly. Then the truth slowly but surely began to dawn on me. I had been rude and unfair to Jane as she proudly cheered me home at the finish, and frankly, I was behaving like a petulant, spoiled child.

This wasn't Jane's fault, and I owed her an apology. Nor was it the course, the hotel, or anything else for that matter. This was my fault, and much as it hurt, I knew it. I'd arrogantly assumed that, after running consecutive personal bests in my previous two marathons, all I needed to do was train like I'd done before, rock up to the start, and run the race a bit faster. If only it were that easy! I'd got my pacing wrong, going way too fast in the early stages of the marathon, and I learned a painful lesson during the race – namely, putting time in the bank does not work. All that leads to is exhaustion closely followed by running out of steam long before the end of the race. And if I were honest – despite what I'd told myself in the lead-up to the race – training had not been all good. My commitment level had dropped, my approach was lackadaisical, and I'd been more than happy to skip the odd tough session. The simple truth was that I was to blame, and the buck stopped with me. If I was ever going to break three hours, I had to start taking this far more seriously, knuckle down, and work harder. The sense of achievement that I'd felt following the London Marathon had been brought crashing back down to earth. I had regressed, and I didn't like it. Time to ask myself, "How much do you really want this?"

# CHAPTER 7

BRIGHTON 10KM, NOVEMBER 2017

It was to be some time before I'd take part in a marathon again, but I was desperate to move on from the memory of the Richmond debacle as quickly as possible. It was time to take the bull by the horns, strap on my race trainers once more, and prove to myself that I could do better! Wanting to shake things up a bit, the race chosen was the Brighton 10km, conveniently located a short drive from home. Organised by the Brighton and Hove Athletic Club, the course follows an out-and-back route along Brighton and Hove seafront, and if lady luck shines, and it's not a windy day, this race has PB potential written all over it. It had been a while since I last ran a 10-kilometre race in anger, so it would be interesting to see how this race panned out.

I had about eight weeks to train for the run, and I figured if I made a few small tweaks to the training plan I'd followed for the Richmond marathon, I'd be able to find the extra speed that a 10km race requires. And so, I shortened and sped up my speed session, and I increased the pace of my tempo runs while, at the same time, decreasing their overall distance. Time to put it all into action and see if my strategy might work.

Race day dawned, chilly but with barely a breath of wind. This, for me, represented ideal conditions. I like running in colder weather, and it often brings out the best in me. Arriving at the race start in plenty of time, I had a thorough warm-up. After all, it was cold, and I'm not getting any younger! Best to warm up my aging muscles before trying to run fast. I lined up on the start line with my fellow competitors, many of whom were looking profoundly serious and ready for the battle ahead. Once we got racing, very quickly I settled into my stride and went to work. 2km in and this felt fast – faster than I'd run for a long time! Nevertheless, I was feeling good and running strong – so far, so good. The course reached its farthest point at the King Alfred Leisure Centre in Hove before turning through 180 degrees and heading back along the promenade. I was working hard by now but still feeling very much in control. 7km in, the route goes back past the start/finish line before runners tackle the final 3km.

The event start is graded, with the rankings determined by the finish time you had predicted when entering the race. I'd estimated finishing in around 40 minutes, and something on my race number (unbeknownst to me) that was pinned to my T-shirt indicated that to the race organisers. Passing the start/finish line, I was well inside my projected 40 minutes. That, in turn, prompted the gentleman who was commentating on the race to say over his microphone, "This runner is having the race of his life!!" Beginning to feel the pace by this stage, his kind words were a real source of encouragement. Another 1500 exhausting metres down the road, and I reached the 180 degrees turn which would lead me back to the end of the race. With legs that were throbbing and lungs feeling like they were about to burst, I headed back towards the finish with 1.5km to go. I could see the finish in the distance and no matter how hard I was running; it just wouldn't get any closer! 800m to go and everything is aching so badly. Something in my head is saying to me, "Just stop!" But something much stronger, more positive is saying, "Don't even think about it! Grit your teeth and run for all you are worth." 400m left to run and the finish line is in sight, just one more big effort and this pain will all be over. That final 400m seemed to take forever. But, with a last flourish, I crossed the finish line setting a new 10k personal best of 37 minutes 2 seconds, knocking nearly 2 minutes off my previous best, that I'd run nearly 5 years earlier. I was shattered and breathless but absolutely elated! I drove home feeling suitably happy and pleased to wipe the slate clean after the Richmond marathon. The sequence of my recent race results read, good race, bad race, good race. It was time to try and break that sequence, once and for all. Oh, and to the chap who was commentating on that day, thank you so much for your inspiring words, just when I needed them!

CHAPTER 8

BRIGHTON MARATHON, APRIL 2018

"I can't do this anymore; it's too hard." These are the words I uttered to Jane, sitting on our kitchen floor, on a cold February evening. I'd just arrived home from another tough training run, feeling shattered. In preparation for the 2018 Brighton marathon, I'd opted to try a new training program. One found in a book I purchased entitled "The Runner's World Big Book of Marathon and Half Marathon Training". Positioned towards the end of the book was something called the advanced marathon plan, and I decided to try and follow it. The plan is designed for runners who have at least 3 years' experience, who've comfortably completed marathons before and regularly log 35-40 training miles per week. "That's me," I thought. "I tick all those boxes." As I uttered those words to Jane, slumped in our kitchen, I was about 9 weeks into a 16-week training program, and the schedule had been relentless and punishing. I'd been exposed to a whole new world of training, and I was struggling to keep up. Usually, I'd run four days a week, but this plan required me to run six. The sessions included a long run, a tempo run, a speed or hill session with an easy run sandwiched between each of those. While the weekly mileage would reach 60 during the peak training period. This was turning out to be harder than I'd imagined, and I was feeling it. As well as that, I'd decided to attempt to improve my overall fitness, and to that end, I'd started a circuit training class once a week. At times, feeling way out of my depth, there were many days during those sixteen long weeks when I had to force myself out of the door to run. I looked forward to my weekly rest day with a passion, let me tell you! But I was desperate to do everything possible in an attempt to break 3 hours for the marathon, once and for all, and no one said it would be easy. As the 16 weeks came to a climax, feeling in the shape of my life, I was 32lbs lighter than I'd been at the 2016 London Marathon, almost 2 years previous. Race day was approaching fast, and I was feeling anxious and excited all at the same time. Time to put all of this hard work into practice. Let's do this!

I'd originally planned to attempt a sub-3-hour run at the 2018 Vienna marathon, the race taking place on the 22nd of April. Jane and I thought that not only would it give me the chance to attempt a sub-3 run amongst beautiful surroundings (around a route that was new to me), but it'd also be an excuse for a few days away in a stunning city! What could be better? That was the plan until I was given the chance to run from the fast start at the Brighton marathon. For those who don't know, the mass start sets off from the edge of Preston Park, adjacent to the main (A23) road. It then circumnavigates the park for around half a mile, involving a couple of tight turns and narrow roads, at a time when the runners are still bunched together. The fast start would commence further back down the A23, before joining the mass start as they turned onto the A23, resulting in a nice, straight, opening few miles to the race. I can't be certain, but this may have been the first year that the fast start had been introduced, and I couldn't turn down the opportunity to take advantage of it. So it was, that on the 15th of April 2018, I'd take my place amongst club runners at the Brighton marathon, fast start. They must have wondered what a little bloke in a T-shirt, with no athletics club logo displayed on it, was doing here!?

Waiting nervously for the race to start, I had many thoughts flying around my head. Was I ready for this? Would I nail my race strategy this time? Could I maintain the pace I'd need for 26.2 miles? Anxiety and fear started to take over, and negative thoughts were beginning to cloud my judgment. I suppose this was only natural; I mean, I'd been in this position before, only to get things very wrong. But this time was different. Looking back over the tough 16-week training plan that I'd followed, I could honestly say to myself, I hadn't missed a beat. Following the program to the letter (or indeed, the mile), I genuinely felt in the shape of my life. The training was done, the conditions were ideal for fast racing, and it was time to focus on getting my race strategy right. I had to stick rigidly to the plan I'd been rehearsing for weeks. "Whatever you do, Ash, do not panic and go off too fast!" I said to myself. Happily, fate was about to make my job a whole lot easier.

Approaching the start were two athletic-looking gentlemen, wearing matching yellow vests, with balloons strapped around their waists! The race information pack had stated that the pace groups available on race day would start at 3 hours 15 minutes. So, I was pleasantly surprised to see two extremely nice chaps heading towards us, who – as it turned out – would be pacing a 3-hour group. This was perfect because it meant I wouldn't have to worry about my speed. Instead, I could put all of that worry in the pacers' hands and just concentrate on maintaining my rhythm and form. Bingo! The race was about to start, and for now, it seemed luck was on my side.

Racing involves a lot of emotion for me, and as I stood there, waiting for the off, my thoughts were focused on the previous two years. I'd come a long way since the London Marathon, 2016. It'd been a tough 24 months featuring many highs and lows, but gradually, I'd improved and here I was, about to have a crack at a new marathon PB. "This has to matter," I said to myself, "I have to be willing to go above and beyond today. If I'm not ready to do that, I may as well go home right now." As I contemplated these feelings, my heart rate increasing with every minute, the countdown to the start began.

BANG! The gun went off, and we were on our way. Before I knew it, we were passing the mass starters in Preston Park. Patiently waiting for their chance to cross the start line, they were kind enough to cheer and clap as we headed for the city. During the first 5 miles of the run, the course follows ring roads that take you in and out of the city centre, and there are always plenty of supporters lining the streets. Cheering loudly, they compete to be heard above the sound of percussion bands beating their drums. Since its inception, the Brighton marathon has grown into a fantastic race that has become a major fixture on the road racing calendar. The marathon always has thousands of vocal supporters spread across the whole route, offering words of encouragement and high fives to all and sundry, and the atmosphere is always electric!

After 5 miles or so, we turned onto Brighton seafront and headed away from the city, towards Ovingdean. Feeling good and in control, I settled into a nice rhythm. It was somewhere near this point that our group was passed by a man wearing a French club vest. As he ran by, I yelled to him, "Bon Chance!" in my best French! "Merci," he replied. Suitably impressed with my linguistic skills, I proudly turned to one of my fellow runners and said, "I just wished him good luck." He looked at me rather quizzically, rolled his eyes, and retorted, "I know!"

As we began to head back towards the city along the seafront road, the throng of supporters got ever bigger and ever louder, and their support really does offer me a motivational boost. Off in the distance, I could see Brighton Pier and the impressive-looking i360 viewing tower. Runners, a little further back on the course, were coming towards us on the other side of the road, heading towards Ovingdean. As our eyes met across the central reservation, there was a real sense of camaraderie among us as we passed each other. This was just fantastic, and I was loving it!

We crossed the halfway point bang on schedule in a little under 1 hour 30 minutes – man, these pacers were doing an awesome job! I'd been taking on fluid at each of the aid stations and consuming an energy gel every four miles, as per my nutrition plan. About a mile after the halfway mark, the route turned inland towards Hove, and still, the streets were lined with ever more cheering supporters. Nearing 16 miles, I happened to notice someone I knew, watching from the side of the road. My buddy, Dan, had been working in Brighton on that day and decided he'd take advantage of it and watch some of the race. With surprise in his voice as I went past, he said, "Hello Ash!" I hadn't told anyone that I'd be running here today, and now, Dan had spotted me. Now I'd been seen, the pressure was really on!

The miles clicked by with our pace being maintained, almost to the second. Feeling awesome, I was still drinking plenty of water and taking my energy gel every fourth mile. As we passed the 18-mile sign, I remembered how my race had started to fall apart at a similar distance during the Richmond marathon. But – so far – there was no sign of that happening today. It was around this stage of the race that I began noticing I was pulling away from the pacers, opening up a gap of about 10 seconds. Initially, I contemplated backing off and letting the group come back to me; instead, I found myself thinking, "You know what, you feel okay, if we just keep this under control, there is no reason why you can't press on a little – just don't push too hard, too soon!" With that in mind and feeling quietly confident, I pushed on.

The only stage of the race where the course gets a little muted and lonely is the approach to the power station in Shoreham near the 21/22-mile point. There is still a smattering of spectators and the odd band – all of whom are such a welcome and inspiring sight – but it does get a bit quieter. As you round the power station, the long, long, 5-mile drag to the finish begins. This coincided with me starting to feel the unrelenting pace, and the notion of 5 miles in a straight line wasn't a wonderful thought! The miles were beginning to drag now, and I was so pleased to reach the 23-mile mark, where the course

WHAT IF?

turns onto Brighton promenade for the final 3.2 miles.

Amongst the cheering spectators on the promenade was my friend, Dan. As I approached him (around 24 miles), I was really beginning to struggle - the shoulders had dropped, and my head was going down. Whether Dan saw that in my face, I know not, and as I went past him, I shook my head as if to say, "I'm done!" Now, Dan is usually a very placid guy, and rarely does he outwardly show emotion – but not today! Today, he looked straight into my eyes and shouted, "RUN!!" What a simple, powerful, and emotive message that was. My head rose up, and I thought to myself, "Is this it? Is this where this all ends? Are you willing to throw away two years of hard work and sacrifice, so close to the end? What did you expect, a walk in the park? This was always going to be difficult." I had come this far, and though every fibre and sinew in my body was begging for mercy, I said to myself, "You can do this, just keep going!"

If I were to maintain the necessary speed required to finish in under three hours, I had to find a way of distracting my mind from the struggle this had become. I'd read somewhere that counting to 100 is a great distraction tactic, so I began to count! So, here I am, in a world of my own, desperately trying to count to 100! Trust me when I say to you that I never made it to the magic 100 because I was so tired, I kept losing my place! But it worked, and suddenly I was passing 25 miles. Within sight of the finish now, I passed my French buddy who was faltering badly. As I went by, I shouted to him, "ALLEZ!" (In case you do not speak fluent French as expertly as I do, it means come on!) Past 26 miles and for the first time throughout the whole race, I began to believe that this might be about to happen, I might just get under three hours. That thought put a bit of speed in my ruined legs and some air in my lungs, and I started to speed up. Approaching the finish line, I got my first look at the race clock, and it shone back in bright red numbers, 2:57 – something. Unbeknownst to me at the time, Jane was shouting at me and fighting back tears as I went past her. In truth, Jane was the one person who knew how much I'd put into this, and I guess it was a release of emotion. She'd been nothing but supportive throughout my journey, and this moment belonged to Jane as much as it did to me. As I passed over that beautiful, gorgeous, and most welcome finish line, I clocked a time of 2:58:05. Finally, I had a marathon time that started with a two.

Dan's one-word motivational message had furnished me with the final boost I needed to make it to the end. My belief was waning when I passed him, and I needed that kick up the backside. Who knows, I might never have made it under three hours without his inspirational shouting! You may have begun to notice how much the support, encouragement, and inspiration from other people seem to crop up a lot during my races. This wouldn't be the last time this happened either.

In the immediate aftermath of the run, I felt an overwhelming sense of relief. There was no punching the air, no tears, just a quiet feeling of satisfaction. I'd been convinced for a while that I was capable of a marathon time of under three hours if I got my race strategy right. Having done it, I was filled with a tremendous sense of contentment. Race medal collected, I made my way to the finish zone exit and met Jane. I gave her a huge hug and simply said, "Honey, we did it! Let's go home." During our journey, my phone kept relentlessly pinging, informing me that my proud Aunt Sue had shared my Brighton marathon story on her Facebook page, tagging me in the post. She couldn't wait to reveal the news to her friends and our family, and as my phone kept beeping, I thought of her smiling from ear to ear, proud as can be. Oh, and what of my new French friend? He crossed the line in under three hours too. "Très bien, mon ami!"

I did go on to run the Vienna marathon a week after Brighton. It was a terrifically hot April day, and in the end, I was glad that this wasn't to be the race where I attempted to get under 3 hours. Instead of the usual single race, there were three races rolled into one in the form of the marathon, a half marathon, and a relay marathon. All three started from the same point at the same time, making for a pretty chaotic race! But it was fun and a wonderful experience, and I finished in just under 3 hours 20 minutes. The race is highly recommended if only for the pre-race pasta party. I mean, where else can you learn the Viennese waltz while tucking into a bowl of delicious pasta? Needless to say, Jane and I had a wonderful weekend exploring the beautiful city of Vienna, without the pressure of a sub-three marathon on our minds!

During March, something far more important than marathon PB's lit up my life. Jane and I got married on the 31st of March 2018, in an intimate ceremony. The wedding took place in a beautiful Scottish castle, and we were accompanied by close members of our families. I'm never particularly comfortable in public situations, and Jane is very aware of that. When my beautiful bride entered the castle, accompanied by a piper playing the apt "Amazing Grace", I struggled to hold my emotions in check. Jane looked stunning. She walked over to me, took my hands and said, "Are you OK?" My heart melted! If ever I needed confirmation that I was marrying the most amazing lady, this was it. On her wedding day when every bride has the right to relish being the centre of attention, Jane's first thought was to ask if I was OK. That moment left me realising just how lucky I was to be marrying this amazing lady and Jane continues to astonish me with her love, understanding, and kindness to this day. I must confess that I'd gone running on the morning of our wedding! Not for any training reason, you understand – this was purely to calm my pre-wedding nerves!

CHAPTER 9

TRAINING

This is probably as good a time as any to discuss training. But before that, let's talk about my race times and personal bests that are mentioned throughout this book. It's vital to understand that the times are relevant only to me, and they are only here to give some bearing to my story. These personal bests only represent my individual achievements (I suppose that's why the word "personal" is so important!). I'm very much of the opinion that time alone isn't a fair reflection of someone's running capability; rather, we should judge ability by the effort that individuals commit to their own running. Let me try and explain.

We all have our physical limits; if that were not the case, then surely all of us would be running sub two-hour marathons! It's my belief that our limits are dependent on factors such as our age, gender, strength, aerobic capacity, the speed that fate has afforded us, and so on. Some of these are adjustable parameters and others are not. If we're trying to reach our running threshold, then our job is to get the best out of the natural ability that fate has handed us. This involves structured, targeted training within the time that we have available to train.

It's important for me to be honest with myself when considering how many hours I'm willing to commit to my running. Not all of us have lots of time to dedicate to training; after all, we all lead busy lives, and some of us don't want to spend large amounts of time running – and that is absolutely fine. Personally, I always want my running to be an activity that enhances my life and never detracts from it.

Ok, so let me explain further what I mean when I talk about running effort with a practical example. If you have ever been lucky enough to run the London Marathon, you'll know that there's a point during the race where runners come across fellow competitors heading towards them on the opposite side of the road. On one side, runners are between 13 and 14 miles, and on the other, between 21 and 22. I've been lucky enough to experience this moment on a few occasions now, and it's a wonderful opportunity to look into the eyes of your fellow runners.

The elites have that steely-eyed, determined look about them, and they are giving all that they have in an effort to be the best that they can be. Then there are the guys further down the field. As I head towards the 22-mile mark, looking across at my fellow runners approaching the 14-mile point, guess what I see? A steely-eyed, determined look in every face, and each wonderful runner giving their all in an effort to be the best that they can be! We may not look quite as graceful, but my gosh, we're trying! What do I conclude from that? It doesn't matter if you're an elite or one of the mid-packers (like me); the times may change, but the effort being exerted remains the same. So, if you're out there giving it your all, you and I are equal, my friend. We are one and the same, and we are an integral part of this running community!

Remember, my three-hour marathon is no better than another's four, five, or six-hour marathon. Each will have required a lot of hard work and determination and is worthy of high praise. And before I compare my race times to anyone else, I remind myself that comparison is the thief of joy!

I hope that all of the above makes sense because I don't want anyone to think that I'm achieving things that they can't. It is my belief that effort and exertion are the ways to judge the runner, who is striving to be the best that they can be, not race times. Of course, all of this is only my opinion, and you might not agree with me. And you know what? That is fine. Because I never said I was right!

Ok, so all of the above assumes that every runner is trying to chase new personal bests, and of course, this isn't always the case. Because the wonderful thing about running is that it represents many different things to many different people, and its most endearing quality is that anyone can do it. Some of us might be looking to improve, but some of us run for other reasons. These might include physical and mental wellbeing, or for fun, for company, or to enjoy the outdoors, to think and to deal with life's little problems or to get away from the stresses that life can create. Or it may well be all of the above and a multitude of other reasons besides.

Personally, I know that running makes me a better person, husband, and father, and that matters more to me than any personal best. It's also worth saying that while I enjoy challenging my limits, I often love to leave the watch at home and run for the hell of it. For me, there's nothing better than a winter run through a beautiful wood feeling mud squelching under my feet, looking up at the trees that have lost all of their leaves for another year, my vision being impaired by the condensed air from my own breath. Or perhaps, an early morning, spring run, watching a beautiful sunrise, surrounded by trees, plants, and shrubs that are waking up and growing once again, following a long winter. On the other hand, ask me if I enjoy running in high winds and pouring rain (the sort of horrible rain that stings your face), and I might not be so keen!

When I'm on holiday, I adore getting up and going for a run before the locals have woken. In my eyes, there is no better way of exploring the sights, sounds, smells, and landmarks of somewhere new. Running really is a beautiful thing, isn't it? For me, it acts as an antidote to life's little problems.

Right, so on to some training. Before we go any further, I feel a disclaimer coming on! I'm not a coach, and I have zero coaching qualifications – heck, I've never even been coached. So, you might want to ignore the rest of this chapter! Actually, you know those training plans that we've all seen. The ones titled "marathon training plan for beginners" or "training plan for intermediate runners". Mine would be known as "marathon plan for those who are muddling through!" Ok, for what it's worth, here we go.

I don't want to get bogged down in lots of facts and figures and why I run certain sessions and for what reasons. There are many books, videos, blogs, coaches, and personal trainers that can do a much better job of explaining that than I ever could. What I do is listen, read, observe, and then incorporate all that I learn into my own training. I also take a great deal of inspiration from other runners across all abilities. There's nothing more motivating for me than to see someone push themselves to be better, faster, go further or taking on a new and daunting challenge and completing it. To improve or to try takes courage which in turn takes determination and willpower and that's genuinely inspiring for me.

What I can tell you is that I've found running consistently to be beneficial and a real aid to improving my performance. I've also learned the importance of running at varying speeds. For years, I was very much a one-pace runner, with only the odd speed session thrown into my training. These days, I try to run a speed or hill session, a tempo run, a long run, and a couple of easy runs each week. These are separated by approximately 2 to 2 ½ minutes per mile from the fastest sessions to the slowest. The easy runs really help aid recovery from the effort sessions, and I try not to run tough sessions on consecutive days. I wholeheartedly believe in the 80/20 running rule, meaning that 80% of my training is done at an easy pace and only 20% is done at speed. My weekly mileage depends on the goal race that I'm aiming for, but I generally average approximately 45-60 miles per week.

Finally, when practicing for a race, I like to replicate racecourse conditions wherever possible, especially during my longer training runs. For example, if I'm running a flat, road marathon, I try to run on tarmac and of course, there is no need to add too many hills to my route, conversely, if I'm preparing for a hilly trail run, I will try to incorporate lots of off-road runs, with plenty of elevation gain. None of this is rocket science; it's ordinary, simple common sense, and I'm not reinventing the wheel.

Below are a couple of additional lessons that I've learned that I'd like to share with you.

It is only a moment!

This has proved to be a massively important lesson for me! Let me give you an example. Close to where I live is a tough hill that I regularly run when I'm training. It's about 1.5 miles long, with the vast majority of it uphill, with the elevation gain getting steeper towards the top of the climb. As I reach the top, I can feel my heart pumping, and the lactic building in my legs. Cresting the hill and reaching level ground, I concentrate hard on how I feel in that immediate moment. It always astonishes me just how quickly I forget the lactic build-up in my legs, and before I know it, my heart rate has returned to normal. That moment that seemed to hurt so much has already been forgotten, and my run has moved on. For me, the lesson is this, no matter how hard things become during a race or training run, the moment will pass, and I will recover. Trust in your ability and drive through those tough segments. Don't let a bad moment ruin your race.

My mind is the greatest weapon in my arsenal!

That's as long as my attitude is right (and sometimes it isn't!). I have to stand on the start line and believe that I'm capable of what I'm about to attempt. If I don't genuinely believe that, then when my legs are begging for mercy, my mind won't be strong enough to overcome that fatigue.

During most races that I've run, there have been many highs and lows. I accept that, and I keep pushing through the tough lows (remember, those moments will pass) and take advantage during the high moments. I train on my own as much as I can, particularly during tougher sessions because I have to be able to motivate myself when no one else is around. That motivation will be required many times throughout a race, and if I haven't rehearsed it during my training, it won't be there when I need it.

For example, if I think I'm tired, I'll feel tired. Or if I think I'm cold, I'll feel cold. Focusing away from negative thoughts and concentrating on positive feelings is vital. Belief in myself and my own ability is the most important weapon I have because success comes from within. I have no special talent; I have to work hard to succeed. And after thirteen years of regular running, and 51 years on this beautiful planet, I'm still setting personal bests across all distances. Think strong, run strong!

Finally, never stop dreaming big, reaching for new goals and never stop believing in the power of you. Because if you don't, who will? I can read as many books as I like and listen to as much advice as I can gather. But only I can bring the best out of myself, and that starts in my own mind. Strong mind, strong runner, strong results!

CHAPTER 10

THE ULTRAMARATHON DOUBLEHEADER, 2018

After all of the stress that came from maintaining a consistent pace, negative splits, and time pressures at the Brighton marathon, I decided it'd be nice to get out on the trails again and leave thoughts of personal bests behind me for a while. This manifested itself in another shot at an Ultra Challenge event in the form of the Cotswold Way Challenge. Because I'd previously entered an Ultra Challenge race, I was offered an extremely generous discount if I entered an additional race during 2018. This being the case, I thought to myself, "Why not enter a second one, for a laugh?" That is how I found myself with a spot in the Jurassic Coast Challenge too (I do love a discount!). The only problem was that these two 100-kilometre races were only three weeks apart! Oh well, in for a penny, in for a pound, as they say.

The Cotswold Way 100km Challenge, June 2018

The Spa city of Bath is magnificent. Its attractive Bath stone architecture and its Roman Baths make it a fitting backdrop for the start of the Cotswold Way Challenge. The 100-kilometre (62-mile) challenge runs from the city of Bath and finishes in Cheltenham, with the vast majority of the route located on a picturesque section of the Cotswold Way. Though I'd visited Bath before, I hadn't ventured onto the Cotswold Way, and I was very much looking forward to the pleasure of running somewhere completely new to me. With an elevation gain of over 2000 metres, this was going to be the toughest race I'd ever attempted.

The start was located opposite the impressive buildings that form the Royal Crescent in Royal Victoria Park. Whereas I'd started the London to Brighton Ultra Challenge in 2017, slap bang in the middle of the start times, on this occasion, I decided to start with the vast majority of the runners in the 6 am start. This was mainly because I was hoping to finish before nightfall, but equally, I was feeling more confident about my own ultra-running abilities. My one previous ultra being sufficient enough for me to consider myself experienced! Naivety is a wonderful thing, don't you think? The race got underway, right on time, and we quickly climbed out of Royal Victoria Park and onto the Cotswold Way. As the route continued to rise out and away from Bath, the views back down towards the city were stunning with Bath looking resplendent, bathed as it was in the early morning sunshine. Aid Station one quickly arrived at Bath racecourse before the route crossed the A46, continuing on through some lovely farmland.

I found myself running with an extremely nice chap called Brendon shortly after the first aid station. We continued running together for miles, reminding each other to keep drinking and taking our salt supplements (to help ward off the dreaded cramp!). We traversed arable fields and farmlands before crossing over the M4 and passing the beautiful St Mary Magdalene's Church in Tormarton. Continuing along the route, we passed Little Sodbury Hill Fort, whiling away the hours with discussions of races that we'd run before and those that were on our respective bucket lists, while we enjoyed the stunning scenery and glorious weather. This truly was long-distance running at its magnificent best. At some point, after aid station three, near the pretty village of Hawkesbury Upton, we began to drift apart, and I found myself on my own for the first time since leaving aid station one. I hoped I'd meet up with Brendon once again, further along the route.

It was great to reach the halfway point at Wotton Sports Centre, where Jane was awaiting my arrival. By this stage of the day, it was beginning to get hot, and I needed to rest my weary legs. Once again, instead of reaching for the pasta that was available, I made the same mistake I'd made at the London to Brighton race in 2017 and headed for the cakes and chocolates! Why I was surprised when I felt sick shortly after resuming my run I do not know! Would I ever learn? On the way to the village of North Nibley, the route passed the incredible William Tyndale Monument. I found a plaque near this extraordinary structure, and it turns out that it was erected in 1866, in memory of William Tyndale who'd translated the Bible into English. They say you learn something new every day, but more importantly for me at this moment in time, the distraction afforded by this magnificent edifice meant that I forgot I was feeling sick!

Forgetting that I'd been feeling unwell was extremely welcome news, and I pressed on along the beautiful Cotswold Way towards the village of Dursley. Beyond the village were stretches of fields and then a short, steep, uphill road section that took me up to Coaley Picnic site and the most stunning views of the race. Looking out from the aid station, on a gorgeous clear day towards the village of Coaley, it was possible to see the Black Mountains in Wales over the horizon. I could've stayed and admired the view for the rest of the day, but alas, I had a race to complete.

The trail continued through Penn Wood before emerging onto a road that passed the pretty All Saints Church in Selsley. Shortly after this, the route turned left and across a field that was occupied by a herd of rather large cows. I have to confess that I'm not particularly good with cows! As I entered the field, they turned towards me, with an inquisitive look in their eyes making me feel rather nervous. Even though I was about 45 miles into the race and feeling somewhat tired by now, I was across that field like grease lightning! Throwing myself over a stile and away from the impending danger, I looked back to see the cows had returned to chewing away on the grass without the slightest interest in this terrified runner! Relieved that my near-death experience was over, I found myself in the town of Stroud. After the peace and tranquillity of woods and stunning views, this was all rather busy.

The route out of the town was via the longest hill of the race. It was a pleasant surprise to come across jugs of squash that had been left outside by a generous homeowner for those taking part in the Cotswold Way Challenge. How nice is that? Talking of hill climbs, you may have noticed that I refer quite often to running throughout these ultra-races. Trust me when I say, everything changes when you reach a hill! Because during ultra runs, it is considered de rigueur to walk the hills – in fact, it is actively encouraged! If you push yourself too hard whilst traversing the tough climbs of a race, you are likely to pay a heavy price for it during the latter stages of the run, in the form of complete exhaustion and fatigue. Personally, I always ensure that I walk uphill with purpose, trying my best not to dawdle!

Approaching the latter stages now, the course continued through the town of Painswick before an uphill climb into Buckholt Woods. This was a long stretch through the trees, and I felt myself feeling weirdly isolated and claustrophobic. The heat in the woods was strength-sapping, and I was glad when they came to an end. My legs were tiring by this point, and I was devoid of energy, so it was a welcome relief to know that I was on the final push towards Cheltenham. The run entered the urban streets of the town, and as I made my way across the pretty Hatherley Park, my watch registered 100km. I remember thinking, they said the run was 100km, so why aren't I at the bloody end yet!? A mite grumpy (clearly), I left the park, and shortly afterward, heard the commotion from the finish area. And then joy of joys, the flags and gantry that signified the end of the run loomed into view. I crossed the line, utterly shattered in 12h 37m, pleased and relieved to reach the end of what had been an epic run. While I enjoyed a lovely cup of tea, it was great to see Brendon cross the finish, just a little way behind me. It'd been a memorable day and a thoroughly enjoyable experience. With only three weeks until the Jurassic Coast Challenge, I needed to recover – very quickly!

*I believe that the current route differs from the 2018 event.

Jurassic Coast 100km Challenge, July 2018

I can promise you that there was little running done between the Cotswold Way Challenge and the Jurassic Coast Challenge. Rest was what I needed, and rest was what I did! It took me about 10 days to recuperate from the Cotswold Way run, and I enjoyed every blessed moment of putting my feet up. Once recovered, I did manage to get out for a few training runs prior to the Jurassic Coast jaunt, and as race day approached, I was feeling in reasonable condition. This was welcome news because I'd been told that there were some monster hills in the first half of the challenge. This one was going to be tough!

Race day dawned, clear and bright, and I joined my fellow runners in Whitecliff Harbourside Park in Poole for the start. After my usual pre-race macchiato, I joined in with the warm-up and as per normal, made a complete pig's ear of it! Hoping that my race would work out better than the warm-up, I took my place on the start line, ready to tackle the 100-kilometre journey from Poole to Bridport.

We set off at 7 am and made our merry way from Lilliput and onto Sandbanks via the coastal road. Once we reached Sandbanks, about 3 miles into the race, everything came to a grinding halt. Why? Because there's a small stretch of water between Sandbanks and South Haven Point, and the only way to cross it is by ferry. As part of the race entry, we were given a ticket for the Sandbank ferry, and I duly boarded our little boat along with a few confused motorists. They must have wondered what all of these people in running clothing were doing, boarding the ferry all at once! Safely across to the other side, we continued along Studland Beach, and it wasn't long before we happened across the second surprise of the run. For those who aren't aware (and I wasn't), there is a section of Naturist Beach located on the Studland Sands. It was quite a surprise to see people wandering around in their birthday suits, I can tell you! There cannot be many races in the world when one comes across this rather unusual sight. Naked bodies behind us, we carried on following the coastal trail before reaching the amazing rock formation at The Foreland. Barely 12 km in and this race was already turning into an epic journey!

The first aid station was positioned in the small coastal town of Swanage, and from there the route turns inland and heads towards the Majestic Corfe Castle. On the way to the castle, the first of the tough climbs that I'd been promised appeared in front of me. Even walking up it was tough, and this was only a taster of what was ahead. Corfe Castle kept disappearing from view as the route went up and down through valleys occupied by flocks of sheep. I'd never seen the castle before, and watching it reappear on the horizon made for an impressive sight. The race route took us around three sides of the castle, but before that, was the second rest stop located behind the heritage railway station in Norden. The station is beautiful and is part of the Swanage Railway. The route actually took in the platform, which was slightly surreal but equally as awesome! The path continued across the country through Stonehill Down nature reserve and Tyneham, and I can promise you that some of the views were breathtaking. The sun was out and no clouds in the sky meant that the views stretched for miles. I was loving every minute of this, and the best was still to come.

As the route returned to the coastline, the views that appeared ahead of me literally took my breath away. This was the first time I'd ever visited the Jurassic Coastline, and it didn't disappoint. I reached the coast via Flower's Barrow, and as I came over the crest of the hill, the view opening up in front of me was spectacular. The sight of the sun shining off the sea was beautiful, and at that moment, almost alone in this breathtaking landscape, I couldn't imagine a more perfect place to be. Looking along the coastal path, my eyes were met with dramatic hills and the magnificent shoreline of the Dorset coast.

Whilst ingesting the spectacular scenery, my mind was rudely returned to the task in hand as my eyes followed the route of the coastal path. In the midst of all this beauty, I'd almost forgotten that I would be running over these very steep climbs that'd overwhelmed my senses! Running down the first hill, the climb ahead appeared to get steeper by the second – this thing looked like a mountain! The path, at times precariously close to the cliff edge, continued over Arish Mell, with its white cliffs and golden sandy beaches. In places, the path was eroded, making the climbing even more difficult. Just walking over the hills was hard enough, and there were times when I came to a grinding halt, gasping for breath! Still, with the epic views surrounding me, I could be taking a breather in worse locations than this!

The path around Mupe Bay beach hugged the cliff edge once again, and watching my step became of supreme importance! Once I'd safely negotiated the trail and reached the bottom of the precipice, the sight of the sun dazzling off the cliffs behind me was incredible. Around every corner, there was another mind-blowing sight, and the rocks of Fossil Forest were no exception. Continuing on, up and down hills and steps, the path led into the charming Lulworth Cove. There were boats bobbing up and down in the bay and lots of people enjoying a gorgeous afternoon on the beach. The route took me around the crescent-shaped beach across the pebbles and sand, passing sunbathers and kids eating ice creams. Though it was getting extremely warm by now, I did manage to resist stealing an ice cream from an unsuspecting child!

My journey continued on past the outstanding beauty of St Oswald's Bay and Man O'War beach before arriving at the awe-inspiring Durdle Door. What a sight this awesome limestone arch is. Though it was extremely busy around here, I managed to get my photo taken, with the impressive view of Durdle Door behind me! After stopping and enjoying the majestic landscape for as long as I dared, I continued on, up yet another steep climb.

By the time I reached the halfway rest stop in Weymouth, it'd turned into an extremely hot day, and the sharp ascents and descents of the proceeding hills had started to have an effect on me. I was hot, hungry, and my legs were pummelled! Instead of heading for the cake (as I had before!), I did the right thing and tucked into some delicious pasta. I needed to restock the energy stores and get some fluid onboard. Staying hydrated was hard work, and I was feeling a little dehydrated when I arrived in Weymouth. But after some food and drink, feeling much better, I set off along the promenade above Weymouth Beach. Weymouth seafront is very pretty with its multitude of guesthouses, kiosks, and sandy beaches, and it's somewhere I must visit again in the future to fully appreciate its quaint English seaside beauty.

There is a little bridge that spans the harbour entrance in Weymouth, and as I arrived there, would you believe it, the bridge went up! After a 5-minute delay, I was on my way once again, leaving the charming town of Weymouth behind me.

The second half of the race was a bit of a blur! The heat and exertion of the day had really got to me, and I struggled from Weymouth onwards. The beautiful views that made up the first half of the run were mostly behind me now, and this section of the Southwest Coastal path was much quieter. The mud that I was running over had been baked hard by the summer sun, leaving the path rutted and difficult to walk and run on. There was no shade from the unrelenting sunshine, and during one particularly tough section, it felt like I didn't see another person for hours.

It was a huge relief to reach aid station 6 at Abbotsbury Swannery. Jane was there, and seeing her smiling lifted my spirits. Whilst enjoying a much-needed cup of tea, I began to contemplate the 18 kilometres that remained. I thought about it and mulled it over with Jane before deciding that if I took my time, I could make it to the end. The sun was fading now, and it was getting cooler, and the worst of the hills were behind me. I just had to keep putting one foot in front of the other. After saying my goodbyes to Jane, I set off feeling tired and somewhat alone.

Things were not about to get easier anytime soon, and shortly after leaving the Swannery, the trail led onto Chesil Beach. And I don't mean behind the beach on a nice smooth path, I mean actually on it! My aching legs were not impressed by the thought of walking along a deep stone beach at this stage of the race! My saving grace came in the form of the walkers I caught up with who'd been taking part in the second half of the Jurassic Coast Challenge. As well as the full 100km challenge, participants can take part in half or quarter distance races, and it was a real boost to my morale to catch up with those walkers who were reaching the latter stages of their journey. Their welcoming, friendly smiles, and words of encouragement were so kind, and I offered my own encouraging words of wisdom to each of them in return.

After what felt like an interminable period of time, I reached the penultimate aid station at the 94km mark – only 6km to go from here. By the way, it was at this rest stop that I discovered the joy and pleasure of pineapple slices! Not only are they delicious, but I've yet to find something that quenches my thirst to a greater degree of unmitigated gratification. If you haven't discovered this delight, I strongly suggest you try it.

The final 6 kilometres meandered through a caravan park and over one more strength-sapping climb before a tough descent finally led us into the town of Bridport… YES!!! The route headed off the coastal path for the last time and onto smooth, forgiving tarmac before reaching the finish, in a field adjacent to a Morrisons supermarket! Finally, after 12 hours and 55 minutes, I'd reached the end of what had been the toughest physical challenge of my life, there can be no doubt about that. It'd been worth it though because, particularly during the first half of the race, the views and scenery I'd encountered had been amongst the absolute best that I've ever witnessed – probably the best ever while running, and I wouldn't have missed it for the world.

As for Ultra Challenge events, if you are looking to take your running beyond the marathon distance, you could do a lot worse than to start here, the challenges are brilliantly organised, the routes well-marked, and the rest stops are incredibly welcoming and well-stocked. All this means that you can just concentrate on enjoying the experience and getting to the end. Trust me, it really is a whole lot of fun!

After all the exertions I experienced throughout the first half of 2018, the rest of my running year was quiet. Jane and I spent a wonderful fortnight together on our delayed Honeymoon. During an amazing two weeks, we crossed the Atlantic Ocean aboard the ocean liner Queen Mary 2, sailing from Southampton to New York. Each day during the crossing, I'd take my morning run on the promenade deck as the ship cut through the sea. It was quite surreal to be running around the ship (3 laps of the promenade deck equalling one mile!) as the beautiful blue ocean passed by.

While we were in New York, I took the opportunity to run around the famous Central Park. What a superb and beautiful place to run that was, and it even has a special lane reserved for runners and walkers circling around the perimeter of the park! A short flight north took us to the final destination of our Honeymoon, the stunning

Niagara Falls in Canada. While we were there, on a beautiful late summer day, I awoke at 6 am and headed out for a run alongside the powerful yet majestic Niagara Falls. Save for the street cleaners preparing for the day's tourists, there wasn't a soul around. It was such a peaceful scene, broken only by the thunderous sound of the water passing over the falls. What an awe-inspiring and breathtaking way to start a new day.

CHAPTER 11

SOUTH DOWNS WAY 50, APRIL 2019

If distance were the parameter, then 2019 was going to be my toughest racing year to date. With that in mind, I'd trained hard, and I felt in reasonably good shape for the South Downs Way 50-mile race. My warm-up races had a familiar ring to them, as in previous years, and in February, I ran the Tunbridge Wells half marathon for the 6th time. This is a fantastic race with its friendly feel and welcoming volunteers. Though the course is largely rural, there are small pockets of supporters in all the right places and the odd band along the way to boost morale. The route itself is a tough one to pace correctly, particularly as large parts of the first half are downhill, and near the midway point comes the infamous, tough climb up Spring Hill. Hard as it is, though, I must enjoy the challenge because it happens to be where I ran my half marathon PB!

In contrast, the Lydd 20-mile race in March is pancake flat. The rural course is run on country lanes that dissect farm fields. There are few hedges and trees around the route to stop the often strong winds that blow across the course, and the 2019 edition of the race was no exception with winds approaching 40mph! There was debris all over the course, and at one point, the route was diverted through a field to avoid a fallen tree! Many people find this a difficult race because there isn't a lot to see and very few spectators on the route. I, on the other hand, love it. It's an ideal opportunity to rehearse Spring marathon race plans and because there are not many onlookers, it is a great chance to practice the art of motivating oneself when things get tricky.

The last of my training races was a new one to me. It was organised by the Coastal Trail Series, and it took place on the South Downs near Eastbourne. Though not much of the route would be included on the South Downs Way 50, it was a perfect opportunity to run on similar terrain. Just like the Lydd 20, the wind was blowing a gale on race day, and it made the already slippery undulations even harder. Incorporated in the course were the Seven Sisters hills on the coastline of Beachy Head. With the wind directly in my face, they were brutally challenging! This was a well-organised race and the perfect preparation for what was to follow.

Once all of the dress rehearsals were over, it was time for the main event – the South Downs Way 50. With 1750m (5700ft) of elevation, this was going to be one tough nut to crack! As you might expect, arriving on race day, I was ever so slightly nervous! The first obstacle I had to negotiate was the pre-race kit check. The event, organised by Centurion Running, has a mandatory kit list and the rules are simple and clear. If you aren't carrying all of the obligatory kit, you don't start the race. I'd packed my race bag over and over again but walking nervously towards the kit check desk, opening my bag, I was certain I would've forgotten something. But today, luck was on my side, and I passed the kit check test with flying colours – hopefully, the race would be this easy!

Looking around the room at my fellow runners, things looked vastly different when compared with what I'd seen at the Ultra Challenge races. With the Ultra Challenge events, there are many more walkers than runners, and this means that you see lots more walking boots, hiking equipment, and big, traditional rucksacks. But here, here there were trail running shoes and racing vests aplenty.

Everyone looked fitter and more relaxed than me, and I was beginning to feel out of my depth.

As a road runner, I'm used to seeing names like Nike, New Balance, and Adidas adorning peoples running attire. Here the names were Inov-8, Ultimate Direction, and La Sportiva – names normally associated with trail running. I'd at least purchased a Salomon race pack for the event, so I didn't look completely out of place. Looking down at the impressive array of trail shoes that were strapped to the other runners' feet and then glancing down at my Adidas Energy Boost road shoes, I felt rather inappropriately dressed. Why was I the only one wearing road shoes? Actually, while I'm on the subject of shoes, it's time for a small confession. Throughout all of the trail races I've taken part in, I've only ever worn trail shoes on one occasion. Maybe it's the road racer in me, but I much prefer the comfort and fit I get from road shoes as opposed to trail shoes. I know that means that I compromise on support, grip, and toe protection, but I guess I like what I like. However, as I became a more experienced trail runner, I soon learned the benefit of a good trail shoe. And these days, when I'm off-road, I'm always in the right footwear.

Back to the job in hand and making my way towards the start, I began to contemplate the 13-hour cut-off time that applied at this race. In the Ultra Challenge runs, I'd effectively had 24 hours to complete the 62-mile course. But today, I had only 13 hours to finish a 50-mile race. This was turning into an ever more daunting prospect by the minute! Before the run got underway, the race director (James Elson) gave us a quick pre-run briefing. While he was talking, he asked if there were any runners joining us today who were new to Centurion races. A few hands went up around me, and I tentatively raised mine. At that moment, my fellow runners began to applaud us, newbies, and a chap stood next to me turned in my direction and said, "Good luck today and welcome to the family." It sounds daft I know, but it was quite an emotional and heart-warming moment and all at once, I found myself beginning to feel much more relaxed and at home.

The race starts near Worthing College, and there is a climb of roughly two miles out of the coastal town before the route reaches the South Downs Way. I was here to learn today, and with that in mind, I'd started towards the back of the 400-strong field, wanting to see how everybody else approached the run and learn from their experience. The race began, and it was time to go to school.

The first climb, immediately after the start, was taken at a nice, steady pace, and I followed suit and did what everyone else around me was doing. This was good because it meant that as we reached the South Downs Way, the gentle tempo meant that I hadn't been stressed at all – lesson one learned! As the course reached the impressive Chanctonbury Ring, I felt good and surprisingly relaxed. It was a chilly morning, but fortunately, there was hardly a breath of wind around, and what little there was came from behind us. The run continued along the chalk paths and on through a pig farm. This was a first for me, having never experienced running alongside a pig farm before! Trust me when I say, the smell was quite interesting and rather pungent!

The first aid station located near Botolphs appeared at 11 miles, and this was to be my first introduction to a Centurion aid station. The delights on offer are best described as a sort of 1980s New Year's Eve buffet, minus the vol-au-vents and the quiche, crossed with a primary school party! There are mini sausage rolls, cocktail sausages, nuts, chocolates, sweets, crisps, cheese, marmite, and peanut butter sandwiches, and plenty more besides, including delicious peanut butter and jam wraps! As well as coke, water, and energy drinks and even tea and coffee at the latter aid stations. But the best thing about Centurion aid stations is the volunteers. Predominantly made up of trail runners, they are the most supportive, encouraging, helpful, and kind bunch of people you will ever meet. Always a blessed relief to see, they have kept me going on many occasions. The beauty of the aid stations on the SDW50 is that they are positioned at the foot of hills. This makes for an ideal time to stock up on goodies and then indulge in a little snack as you traverse the next hill. Fully stocked up after my brief stop, I munched my way up and over Truleigh Hill.

The route continues along the chalk paths, up and down rolling hills, and there are some great views inland as well as over towards Brighton and the coast. On past Devil's Dyke and through the second aid station at Saddlescombe Farm, I ran, chatting happily with my fellow Centurions and admiring the views. Shortly after leaving Saddlescombe, the course crosses over the A23 via a bridge near Pyecombe. Merrily minding my own business and about 24 miles into the race, it was at this point I fell flat on my face! I didn't fall over a rock or stone that was protruding from the ground resulting in a dramatic trail running tumble; instead, I decided to trip on a curb as we passed over the bridge. So much for being a roadrunner! A couple of runners who were with me stopped to check that I was ok. But with dented pride and trying to be very masculine (despite the fact my thumb hurt like hell), I jumped up in a flash and said, "I'm fine." In truth, there was no real damage, but my thumb was cut and if you have ever cut yourself while running, you will know that it won't stop bleeding! Maybe it's because your heartbeat is raised or something. But whatever the reason, it's a nightmare to stop the blood flow. Of course, it did stop in the end and left me with that horrible, sticky feeling on my hands for the rest of the run. The joys of being a clumsy runner!

Onwards I trudged, passing through the aid stations at Housedean Farm and then Southease. Over hills, through a small wood and past umpteen sheep meandering along, and before I knew it, 34 miles were behind me. Feeling ok, I was enjoying the views, but the downhill sections had brought with them an unexpected new phenomenon. The descents were putting a lot of pressure on my quadriceps, and the declines were becoming harder than the ascents. At least on the ups, you could walk – in fact, walking the inclines is very much recommended when one is ultra-racing – but along the flat and downhill passages of the race, I wanted to try and run. It turns out that when it comes to ultrarunning, the descents become as tough – if not tougher – than the ascents!

After passing the towering Firle Beacon mast, I met Jane at the Bo-Peep aid station. It was great to receive a hug and a kiss from her and a delicious granola cookie to fuel the next few miles. The approach to the historic village of Alfriston involves a long descent, and making my way down the hill, my quads were killing me, every step sending sharp pains through my thighs! After a brief stop and a glass of coke at the Alfriston rest stop, I began starting the climb out of the village, hands on knees, trying not to look up at the long rise ahead of me. In the distance, I could see a fellow runner making his way up the hill, and by the time I'd reached the final rest stop of the race, at Jevington Village Hall, we were side by side. Leaving the village almost at the same time, the very first thing I did was lead the poor chap the wrong way! Quickly realizing my mistake, I apologised profusely, and it wasn't long before the two of us were starting the last climb of the race together. Looking back, this was a special moment for me. Two broken men, who'd never met before this moment, chatting about their race experience and how much everything was hurting by this stage. I never did find out my companion's name, but our conversation as we struggled up this chalky hill made the ascent so much easier. These are among the little moments that make ultrarunning so special.

Reaching the crest of the last hill was such a relief! From there I had to navigate my way down a tricky ravine, affectionately known as the gully. It's incredibly narrow and uneven, and the path narrows into a V shape underfoot. All of this makes it very treacherous, and I was glad when I reached the end of it and found my feet back on tarmac footpaths. The run towards Eastbourne College was fun, and the race finishes with a lap of the college athletics track. What a blast this had been. Though I was exhausted, I had really enjoyed my first Centurion race. I'd met some wonderful people, enjoyed some stunning views, and eaten plenty of guilt-free party food! But, if I thought this one was tough, things were about to get a whole lot tougher.

CHAPTER 12

LONDON MARATHON, APRIL 2019

Well, that was a bit of a shock! Three weeks after completing the South Downs Way 50, it was London Marathon time again. You've probably realised by now, this is one of my favourite races on the calendar, and this was to be my 8th time running around the streets of the capital. To date, I've completed the course dressed as Bananaman, Buzz Lightyear, in a rather sexy pink tutu, and sometimes, I've even taken part in shorts and a t-shirt! Having recently raced over fifty miles and not feeling fully recovered, I wasn't expecting much from this run. My plan was to start fairly conservatively and hopefully finish around the 3-hour 10-minute mark. That was assuming the weather would be on my side, and waking up on race day, I opened the curtains to see clear skies and no wind. Stepping outside yielded even better news; it was only about 12°C – perfect running weather for me.

Having had my normal race day breakfast consisting of porridge and a banana, accompanied by lashings of coffee, Jane and I set off for the now familiar drive to Blackheath. Having driven it so many times by this point, I think we might be able to drive it blindfolded! (Warning: do not try this at home, that would be stupid!). We arrived, parked in our usual spot, and started our customary walk. On the way to the start, we always stop for an invigorating coffee, and our favourite haunt is Madeleine's Creperie. If Madeleine's isn't open, our second choice is The Italian Brasserie. My preferred weapon of choice is a strong macchiato – ideal pre-race fuel and a big caffeine hit! We like to arrive early so that we can soak up the atmosphere around the start. I like to watch the proper athletes going through their warm-up routines. On this occasion, Mo Farah was looking particularly cool in dark shades, a cap, and something that resembled a shell suit. He acknowledged the watching crowd as they offered words of encouragement, wishing him good luck for the race.

I took my place in the green start and waited eagerly for the race to get underway. I endure rather than enjoy these final moments of anticipation, and I often find myself contemplating the idea of feeling physically fine and raring to go before the start, and knowing that in a few hours' time, I'll cross the finish line feeling physically broken and mentally exhausted. Am I the only one who loves this thought? There is nothing better than giving my all to the race, knowing I'll have the pain in my muscles to prove it by the end! There is something personally – and weirdly – satisfying about that.

The race got going, and I quickly settled into my stride. There are actually three starts at the London Marathon consisting of a blue, red, and green zone. The blue and the green starts merge shortly after the race gets underway and they then join the red route runners between the two and three-mile section. I've no idea how long it's been the case but ever since I've run here, there is a fun tradition where, as the starts merge, both sets of runners can be heard booing each other! Of course, it's all done in jest, and it always makes me smile. As we passed the four-mile marker, one of the three-hour pacemakers passed by me, along with his small army of runners, all trying to get round in under the magic 3-hour time. (I read somewhere that by the end of the race, only about 10% of those who start with a pacer actually finish with them.) Anyway, as they ran by me, for a split second, I almost went with them. Instead, I slapped my wrist and said, "No, Ash – you have your own plan today – let them get on with their race and you stick to yours."

At a pleasingly metronomic and consistent pace, I continued past the Royal Artillery Barracks, the Old Royal Naval College, the Cutty Sark, the endless bands, and the deafening noise emanating from the thousands of spectators who line the streets of London, shouting encouragement to perfect strangers, as if they were old friends. Passing other runners, one can't help but notice many of the messages and photos adorning their running vests, such as: "For Dad" or "In memory of." There were large numbers of charity vests on show too, confirming that lots of people running here today are raising much-needed funds on behalf of many diverse charities. I found myself contemplating the umpteen personal reasons that've brought my fellow runners to this race, hoping they all achieve their dreams. Looking ahead of me to see thousands of heads bopping up and down, it felt like I was swimming in a sea of humanity. Much that is good about the human race was on display here today. The organisers, the volunteers, the crowds, and the runners all brought together to be part of this wonderful event. These thoughts were beginning to make me feel quite emotional.

Passing over Tower Bridge and on towards Canary Wharf, I was feeling okay and enjoying my run until suddenly I began to get a strange feeling in one of my calf muscles. It began building into awful pain that runners know all too well – I could sense the dreaded sensation of cramp rearing its ugly head! What to do? I could stop, stretch the leg, and see if that helps. Or I could change my running gait and cadence. Maybe speed up a bit. I was probably paying the price for attempting to run a marathon only three weeks after completing a fifty-mile race; my body still fatigued. In the end, I decided to up my pace a tad. Feeling strong (except for the cramping sensation) I figured that this might be a symptom caused by the flat profile of the course and the consistent pace that I'd been running. As the miles ticked by, surprisingly the plan seemed to be working. Every so often, feeling that uneasy twinge of cramp manifesting itself in my calf, I reacted by speeding up a little, and it seemed to stop that nasty spasm in its tracks.

Reaching the Embankment, it was great to spot Jane near Cleopatra's Needle. I gave her a quick thumbs up and pressed on with only a few miles to go from here. Shortly after passing Jane, I began to make out a familiar sight ahead of me. Drawing closer, I could see that it's a flag, attached to one of the three-hour pacers who'd passed me earlier in the race! Clearly, I must've been speeding up more than I'd realised. All of a sudden, I had a new goal – could I get under three hours at the London Marathon! I'd dreamed of doing it on many occasions; could that dream become a reality? Racing up alongside the pacemaker, I soon passed him. Once he was behind me, I remember saying to myself, "Whatever happens now, DO NOT look back! There was no comfort in looking backward; all I could do is look forwards and keep running." Buoyed by this unexpected turn of events and no longer thinking about cramp, the only thing on my mind was to focus, stay strong, and keep going. Fuelled by an intoxicating mix of adrenaline and exhaustion, I swung right past Big Ben and onto Birdcage Walk. The spectators were making their voices heard now, leaning over the barriers that separate runners from supporters. The noise here is always deafening, and they cheer runners' home like heroes. By now, tired and praying for the finish, I started to mutter under my breath, cheesy, inspirational quotes. You know the sort of thing, "This is your time, Ash. Pain is temporary, glory lasts forever," etc., until I could take no more, and I tell my inner voice to shut up already; I'm busting my balls here! I run with my heart on my sleeve; I have to be emotionally involved, and at that moment, I couldn't think of anything other than getting under three hours. Past St James' Park and desperately resisting the strong urge to check over my shoulder – "just keep running!" Turning past

Buckingham Palace, I saw the finish on The Mall, but my blurred vision couldn't see the race clock yet. Abruptly it dawned on me that the pacemaker might have started behind me. If he crossed the timing mats at the start after me, I might be ahead of him on the road, but not in terms of race time! Where was that damn clock!? At last, I could see it, and I fixated hard on the numbers. As they focus into view, I can make out 2:58! Running as if my life depended on it, sprinting for all I was worth; I crossed the finish line in… 2:59:28! I couldn't believe it; I'd just broken three hours at the London Marathon. This really was an unexpected result, and if I hadn't started to feel the onset of cramp, who knows, this might never have happened! Crossing the finish line, I asked a gentleman who had just completed his race if I could give him a hug! I was so elated, and this was a moment I wanted to remember; I just needed to hug someone.

On tired legs, walking past the rows of baggage lorries, I found the one displaying the numbers that corresponded with my race number. Bag collected, I make my way under Admiralty Arch and across the road towards Trafalgar Square to meet Jane. I couldn't wait to see her, and when our eyes met, she ran towards me and gave me a massive cuddle and a big kiss! With the wonders of modern technology – and the London Marathon app – Jane already knew my race time, and she was buzzing! We boarded the train back to Blackheath to collect our car, picked up a celebratory coffee on the way, and made our way home. I suspect that by the time we had reached the end of our journey, she was fed up with hearing me mention that I'd finished the London Marathon in under three hours! Little did she know that I wouldn't stop talking about it for days!

So, who acted as a massive inspiration at this race? Well, that honour has to go to the three-hour pacer whom I passed on the Embankment. Unbeknown to him, catching up and passing his group gave me the impetus I needed for that final push to the end. Had that not happened, I'm not sure I would've been able to find the extra speed that I needed. Thank you very much, Mr. Pacer, whoever you are!

A few weeks after the London Marathon, Jane and I took a trip to the Lake District to take part in a couple of races organised by the Keswick Mountain Festival. The fun takes place over a weekend in May and entails various races on foot, along with swimming and cycling events, and as well as the exercise elements, there's also music and plenty of delicious food. On Saturday, I took part in a 25-kilometre trail run that circumnavigated Derwent Water. The race route takes runners up and over rocky trails and boulders, past rivers, woods, and shore paths. Along with the Jurassic coast, this is the most stunning landscape that I've ever had the pleasure of running through. The views from up in the hills, back across Derwent Water and the surrounding countryside were truly spectacular and it's a reminder of just how beautiful England is. On Sunday, Jane and I both completed the 10k trail race, and I imagine that the access to the start is potentially unique, if not exceedingly rare. Because to get to the start, you have to take a boat ride across Derwent Water! The route takes in some gorgeous trails and also the hill known as Catbells before returning to the Festival village in Keswick via beautiful woodlands. It was great to be able to run with Jane. Training for marathons and ultra-races can be time-consuming and it takes me out of the house, often for hours at a time. Over the last five years, Jane has been nothing but supportive during the endless months of training. She often provides a shoulder to cry on, being the first one to hear race news, good or bad, as I cross a finish. Without Jane's endless love and patience, my journey over the last five years would've been considerably harder. Sharing the fun of that 10k race on the magnificent trails that travel around Derwent Water was wonderful, and we had a blast!

CHAPTER 13

SOUTH DOWNS WAY 100, JUNE 2019

"What am I doing here? I can't do this." Those were the thoughts that occupied my mind standing in Matterley Bowl, near Winchester, awaiting the start of my first 100-mile race. If I thought I was out of my depth at the South Downs Way 50, this was a whole new level. The Centurion Running South Downs Way 100 travels from Winchester in Hampshire to Eastbourne, East Sussex. And with 3800m (12700ft) of ascent, this would be by far and away my toughest running challenge to date. I'd entered the event nearly a year ago, and this day had been at the forefront of my mind ever since. And here I was, finally waiting to begin this epic (or should that be ridiculous) challenge. My training for the race had gone OK (though being new to this distance, it was all a bit of a learning process, and in all honesty, I hadn't a clue!). I'd experienced my first back-to-back long runs (that is lengthy runs on consecutive days) and spent some time running on coastal trails. Had I done enough? I wasn't sure, but I guess we were about to find out.

Jane and I travelled to Winchester, the day before the race, on a wet June day. The closer we got to our destination, the harder the rain fell, and by the time we arrived in Winchester, it was of truly biblical proportions. This was not exactly what I'd been hoping for, but this was an English summer after all! After a very restless night and little sleep, race day arrived all too quickly. One final kit check, some breakfast, and a prayer, and it was time to make my way to the start.

I could hear the race briefing going on, but I wasn't really listening; instead, my eyes were moving from one fit-looking runner to the next. Everybody else seemed to be relaxed and laughing as we waited for the klaxon to sound, and the race to start. As I scanned my fellow runners, my eyes came upon a lady I thought I recognised. Her name is Gwen, and I didn't really know her that well. She is a friend of Jane's, and we'd never been properly introduced. But sort of knowing someone was enough for me, and I hurried towards her, introduced myself, and promptly gave her a hug! I needed to release my nervousness, and that cuddle really helped. We both agreed that what we were about to attempt was ridiculous and plain silly - just being here bordered on madness! Suddenly out of nowhere, our conversation was broken by the sound of the horn, and ready or not, we were off!

Just like at the South Downs Way 50, I'd decided to start near the back of the pack so that I could learn from the experience of those in front of me. Many of the runners here today were vastly more experienced than me, and I wanted to continue my burgeoning education and learn more about the art of ultra-running, and then try to run my race accordingly. Shortly after the race got going, we came across our first hill of the day, and what had been a run quickly became a walk. This was the way my fellow runners were approaching the task, and so I did exactly the same. The early miles of the race unfolded in much the same vein, and we soon arrived at the first aid station, around 10 miles into the run. My pre-race nerves had settled by now, and it was great to see the enthusiastic and smiling Centurion volunteers. A very brief stop, and I was moving once again. I found these early race miles a bit of a struggle. I think maybe coming from a road racing background, this constant run, then walk was breaking my usual rhythm. During a shorter road race, the norm is to keep running, but ultra-racing is a vastly different animal. I understand that now, but at the time, I found this staccato progress quite difficult to come to terms with. Yes, I'd walked the very steep sections of the Cotswold Way and Jurassic Coast challenges, but we were walking much shallower hills here. But then the people around me knew much more about 100-mile races than I did, and I was here to learn. Those lessons would go on to serve me well in the future. But for now, I was somewhat frustrated, and though I'd known that this run would take many hours to complete, the reality of those several hours were now beginning to dawn on me. Was I really cut out for this sort of distance? All this meant that by the time I reached checkpoint two, at the Queen Elizabeth Country Park near Horndean, I was in a bit of a grump! This was the aid station where I'd see Jane for the first time. The organisers behind the SDW100 – Centurion running – allow the entrants of their events to be crewed at various predetermined parts of the course. This is great because you can stock up on your food and drink etc but more importantly for me, it's a huge morale boost to see a familiar face. I was now about 22 miles into my run, and as Jane and I met, she excitedly said, "Well done, Honey," and asked me how my race was going. I abruptly replied with something along the lines of "I'm not enjoying it, and I'm never doing this again!" Bless her, she didn't know what to say. I had something to eat and drink, barely said another word and set off again.

As I left Jane and the aid station behind me, I started to think and question my attitude. My wife was here today for one reason only – to support me. Jane had welcomed me at checkpoint two with a smile and a kind word, and all I'd done was moan. Nobody had forced me to sign up for this thing, least of all Jane; this had been my choice, and the least I could do was show Jane the gratitude she deserved. I couldn't wait to see her again so that I might apologise for my rude and unnecessary behaviour. This moment proved to be a real turning point for me. It was time to stop sulking, stop feeling sorry for myself, change my attitude and get on with this thing.

The race had started under grey skies, and it had been cold enough to begin the run wearing a jacket to keep out the chill. But by late morning, it was warm enough for just a t-shirt. Because of the rain that had fallen during the previous day, I'd taken the decision to start the run wearing off-road shoes. However, I didn't feel comfortable in them, and I changed into my trusty road shoes at the second checkpoint. The forecast had predicted rain, and sure enough, about 25 miles into the race, the heavens opened. It wasn't persistent rain; rather, it came in the shape of annoying showers. The type of brief downpour where one gets out a rain jacket from his backpack and no sooner has he put it on, blow me, the rain stops! This continued for around 10 miles until I reached the aid station at Houghton Farm. "I am so sorry, sweetheart," were my first words to Jane. She was there, waiting at the checkpoint, ready to feed me and refresh my drink bottles. I felt rightly guilty for my bad mood earlier. I reassured her that I felt fine and that I'd come to terms with the challenge that lay before me, and relentless forward progress was the only objective on my mind.

Houghton Farm is followed by one of the first long hills of the run. The South Downs Way does not have many steep hills; instead, it has lots of long rolling hills. Striding with purpose up the hill, I ate some food and chatted with my fellow runners who were surrounding me. About 45 miles into the day, and I was feeling surprisingly good. The race continued to Amberley and then a massive climb out of the village. As I reached the crest of the hill, I passed a runner and inquired as to how he was doing. An old ankle injury had reared its ugly head, and the poor chap was going to have to call it a day at the halfway point. I felt bad for him and thought about how tough it must be to go through the difficult months of training leading up to this race, only to pull out because of an injury. I wished him well and said that I was sure he would be back to try again another day.

Washington aid station marked the halfway point of the race, and it was great to see it! However, I wasn't stopping here for long because Jane was only a mile or so down the road, and she had a change of clothes and some food waiting for me. When I reached her, we celebrated completing the first half of the race, and I changed all of my clothes, right down to my underwear. For me, it is not only a comfort thing; psychologically it makes me feel like I'm starting all over again. While changing, I didn't sit down once. Before the race, I made the decision that no matter how tired I got, I would do my absolute best to resist sitting down. I feared that if I did, I'd never get up again! With a hug and a kiss, I left Jane behind and started the next climb. Reaching the peak of the hill all of a sudden, I recognised where I was. This was the point where the South Downs Way 50 had joined the South Downs Way. Oh, Happy Day! I can't begin to explain how wonderful it was to recognize my surroundings for the first time during the race. This meant that I would soon be passing through the pig farm and on to Devil's Dyke. It was late in the afternoon by now, and I'd been on the go since 6 am, but the recognition of this familiar sight had given me a new lease of life. Onwards and upwards, time to keep on moving forwards.

The checkpoint at Botolphs (just beyond the pig farm) came and went, and I started the climb up Truleigh Hill. I walked the climb with some fellow runners, and one of them happened to look down at my feet. "They look comfy," he remarked, as he looked at my road shoes. His trail shoes were causing him some discomfort by this stage. Once over the hill, the course continued to Ditchling Beacon where I would see Jane again. A quick chat, a cookie, and a refill of my bottles, and I was away. By this point, I was reaching an incredibly significant juncture in my race. Because I was approaching the 70-mile mark where I'd meet up with my pacer. From the 50-mile

WHAT IF?

point of the race, the good people at Centurion running allow their runners to be accompanied by a pacer, and I was really looking forward to some company. I considered myself incredibly lucky as my running companion for the last 30 miles of the race was not only an extremely accomplished ultrarunner, but he is also a good friend. His name is Paul, and he's run many ultra-distance races in the past, and he'd kindly offered to be my guide for the latter stages of the SDW100. Before reaching Paul, I went through the next aid station at Saddlescombe Farm. Standing at the checkpoint munching down on a cheese sandwich or two, one of the volunteers noticed that my water bottles were full. "I don't like the look of those," she remarked, "are you sure you are drinking enough?" I assured her that I'd been drinking plenty during my travels and my wife had filled my bottles for me at the last crew point, only 1.5 miles ago. I mention this because I think it's a fine example of the care and attention shown by the Centurion race volunteers. This wonderful lady had probably been at Saddlescombe Farm for many hours by that point, and yet she still observed my full bottles and expressed her concern to me. It's this sort of support that blows my mind, and I never take it for granted. Without volunteers who willingly give up their time, events like this couldn't happen. I left that aid station with a smile on my face, feeling good about the world and the people in it.

Up and over another hill and through Pyecombe golf course before arriving at Clayton Mills where I would be happily meeting Jane and Paul. My legs were beginning to feel the distance by this stage, and some conversational distraction was just what I needed. But, having reached the point where we would all meet, something was wrong. No one was there, there was no sign of Jane or Paul. This was a disaster, the nightmare scenario! After a moment of panic, I pulled out my phone from my backpack and phoned Jane. No Answer. What do I do now? Quickly I decided that I couldn't wait, standing around would be the last thing my tired legs wanted, I needed to keep moving. I wrote out a quick text message for Jane, and just as I was about to send it, I heard a familiar and very welcome voice. It was Jane, walking towards me with Paul by her side. What a relief! It turned out that there was some confusion with timings, and they weren't expecting me to arrive so soon, and they had been waiting in the car. None of that mattered to me; all I knew was that I was going to get a much-needed hug from my wife and Paul's company, right when I needed it.

That moment, which went from fleeting panic to a sinking feeling to elation, was quite something. What had been a potential catastrophe turned to jubilation in a flash, and it had certainly focused my mind. Paul was with me now, and as the first sign of dusk began to settle around us, we pressed on towards the Housedean Farm checkpoint, near Falmer. A quick chat with the guys and a couple of sausage rolls later, and we started the climb out of Housedean. Looking over my shoulder, we were treated to the most amazing sunset. You know the sort of thing, that gorgeous orangey, red glow that is sometimes seen on early summer evenings. It indeed was something to behold, and I said to Paul, "Where else in the world would you rather be, right now?" It was a truly special moment on a very special evening. Changing tack slightly, and I'm sorry to be graphic, but it was around this time that I became acutely aware that I needed the loo – and I don't mean number ones! I seemed to remember reading in my pre-race blurb, at the next aid station near Southease, they had toilets. There was the small matter of 7 miles to said aid station to overcome, but I was sure that if I thought about something else other than the call of nature, I'd be fine! Up and over the South Downs Way hills we went, and after what seemed like an age, we arrived at Southease. "Excuse me," I said to a lady behind the food tables. "Where are the loos?" She indicated that they were just around the corner, and I headed in that direction as fast as my legs would carry me! Race disaster number two – the toilets were shut! Things were getting desperate now, and there was nothing for it. I found a bush, hidden from everyone else, and did what I needed to do behind the foliage! The sense of relief was palpable, and it was just in the nick of time!

Returning quickly to racing matters, it was dark and chilly as we left Southease, and Paul and I had resorted to wearing head torches. For the last 5 miles or so, I'd begun to feel cold. I was only wearing a T-shirt, and Paul had been repeatedly asking if I was warm enough, and I'd continually replied "yes." All I was thinking about was getting to the finish as quickly as possible. Of course, this was a rookie mistake, and by the time we reached Jane at the next crew point, I was freezing and shivering and feeling exhausted and demoralised. With only 11 or so miles to go, I felt done in. I turned to Jane and said, "I can't go any further, I need to stop here." I meant it too. In that moment, I couldn't imagine reaching the end, even though I'd completed nearly 90% of the race. The finish seemed impossibly far away. I needed to get warm, quickly, so Jane and Paul got my backpack off and started to put a warm top on me. The daft thing was I couldn't get my left arm above shoulder height! For some reason, it had seized up, and if I tried to raise it, it was agony. Paul and Jane ignored my howls of pain and managed to get the thing on. Together they convinced me to try and go a little further. Paul was fully aware of the fact that I had to get some heat moving around my body again, and he insisted that we try and jog what was a fairly flat and downhill section of the course. Paul is an amazing pacemaker. Actually, a pacemaker is a very loose term for describing his role. Paul took charge of all race management for me. He knew when to let me walk and when to encourage me to try and push on. He became my eyes through the darkness, and he spoke to me endlessly to distract my mind from the pain and exhaustion that was continuing to build up as the race went on. If the path underfoot was uneven, he guided me over the rough terrain, and where it was possible, Paul left me with the smooth side of the path while he took the bumpy side. He was and is the most amazing person to have alongside you when the miles are taking their toll, and I'm forever in his debt. We had barely left Jane behind, and I was feeling fine again; it was as if that moment of real doubt had never happened. As Paul and I descended towards the quaint village of Alfriston, all was good in my world once again.

There are only two more hills to tackle after Alfriston, and standing in the church hall aid station, eating some sweets and drinking a coke, I began to believe – for the first time – I might actually finish this thing. We walked the chalk path up and away from Alfriston and crested the hill, where I was happy to continue walking, but Paul gently persuaded me to jog! Down into Jevington, where I bypassed the final aid station (with four miles to go, I just wanted to keep going), and we climbed the final slope. From the crest of the hill, you can look down over Eastbourne, and shining right back at you are the lights illuminating the athletics track where the race finishes! Down through the same gully found during the latter stages of the South Downs Way 50, the path emerges onto the streets of Eastbourne. As we reached the outskirts of the town to find streetlights burning brightly, we switched our head torches off, and from nowhere, I found my running legs again. I suspect that it had something to do with the fact that the finish was only two miles away, but whatever the reason, I was running again! As we passed the suburban houses, I found myself heading for a perfectly manicured hedge. Ever observant, Paul reminded me to watch my step. Not only has Paul been a light through the darkness, but he's also been a constant source of motivation, encouraging me to find the strength from within to keep pushing. There will be no hero's welcome for him at the end, no finishers buckle, but right here, with only one mile to go, he is my hero. "These hedges are the only things that are holding me up now!" I replied to Paul's concern. Past Eastbourne hospital and less than a mile to go. Speed increasing, we quickly ate up that last mile and found ourselves at the entrance to Eastbourne college. Across the car park, and onto the gorgeous, soft, forgiving, springy track for the final 300m. What had been an epic journey of discovery was coming to an end, and best of all, Jane was there to finish the final lap with me. From the moment I'd entered this race, my goal was to finish in under 24 hours. The award for completing a 100-mile Centurion race is a belt buckle. The buckle has its origins in the Western States 100-mile race in the USA. That race was originally completed on horseback by cowboys until one man completed the distance on foot after his horse went lame. That is the story I was told, anyway! I guess the link to cowboys is why the prize is a belt buckle. Centurion running offers two different finishers buckles – one says on it 100-mile finisher and the other says 100-mile one day. The South Downs Way 100 has a 30-hour cut-off, but I was desperate for that one-day buckle. If I got the run right, I thought I could do it. In the end, I crossed the line in 19 hours, 51 minutes, and 58 seconds. The final lap was brilliant, and it was great to cross the finish line with Jane by my side – the best race crew in the WORLD! Oh, and I didn't sit down throughout the whole race!

I had a couple of other family members watching me finish, which, considering this was around 2 am, is pretty impressive, and it was wonderful to have them share this special moment with me. I had seen my Auntie Sue and my cousin Lucy, but until he was pointed out to me, I hadn't spotted my dad. My Father and I don't have a particularly tactile relationship, and though we love each other, we never really say it. We're men after all! But here today, at the end of my 100-mile journey, my dad gave me the biggest hug ever, and he was determined not to let go! Bless him, he was beaming with pride. If you have ever seen Indiana Jones and the Last Crusade, you may remember a scene in which Doctor Jones Snr thinks he has just lost his son over a precipice. Once he realizes that Henry Jones Jnr is alive and well, he hugs him, and young Jones responds with the face of a child who has found himself in the best place in the World, safe in the sanctuary of his Hollywood Father's arms. My Father and I shared the same sort of hug, and I loved it! But this was no movie hug; this was real, and I didn't want it to end. That wonderful moment made the whole thing worthwhile, and I shall treasure it forever.

And what of Gwen? She gave the race her all, showing true grit and determination, even when a painful, crippling injury struck. Gwen soldiered on, beyond 80 miles before the pain became too much, and she had to pull out. But she is tough, and I know that she'll be back to conquer the South Downs Way 100.

Once the dust had settled, and my family had gone home, leaving Jane and me talking over our epic day, I decided I needed the loo. Getting up from my chair, I crossed the room and made my way into the toilet. I was only in need of a wee, but I decided it might make life easier if I were to sit down (if only for the rest!). BIG mistake! I managed to get up, but as I started to move, I found that my groin had completely seized up. It was a bizarre moment, to say the least. Yes, my legs were sore, and walking was a struggle, but now I was welded to the spot. Managing to get out of the loo, I made my way across the room and back to Jane. I was moving so pitifully slowly; it prompted a medical team sitting nearby to get up and check that I was ok. I reassured them that, apart from an increasing stiffness, I was fine, and Jane appeared to prop me up, just as she had done all day. As I was already standing, we considered it best to try and get back to our car. I do not jest when I tell you that our car was only a 300-metre walk from our current location, yet the walk took about twenty minutes. And the curb that I had to negotiate on the way suddenly felt like the toughest step of the day! Jane managed to wrestle me back in the car, and we started our journey home. Bear in mind that while all this is taking place, Jane has been awake for the same length of time that I had. She must've been exhausted, and yet she was so patient and understanding. I'm embarrassed to say that the moment I was in the car, I fell asleep, and the next thing I remember was Jane waking me up when we arrived home. Struggling indoors, I made it into the shower. Though I still had my calf guards on that I'd worn throughout the race because I didn't have the strength to pull them off – I ended up climbing into bed with them on! As my head hit the pillow, looking forward to a nice, long rest, I was asleep within seconds.

After a few weeks of gentle recovery, I took part in the Centurion Running, Wendover Woods, 50km (31m) night run. The race consists of 3 laps of a 16.5km loop around Wendover Woods in Buckinghamshire. The route travels through some beautiful woods and open fields, and the race has a total elevation gain of some 6000ft (1800m)! This represented the greatest rate of climb that I'd ever attempted during a race, and boy was it tough. One of the hills had a gradient of 1:4! An 11 pm start made for something quite different and unique in my running life, and there was a fun atmosphere surrounding the whole event. My greatest race memory was becoming aware of birdsong filling the air and looking up to see that dawn was breaking. I guess it must've been about 4:30 am. Surrounded by nature, only hearing the beautiful, unspoilt, dawn chorus was music to my ears, and it's a moment I will treasure forever. Unlike those darn hills, which I tried my best to forget!

The Autumn months of 2019 consisted of a couple of very scenic races. In September, I ran the Rye Ancients 30k race. A beautiful route around the Sussex towns and villages of Rye, Iden, Northiam, Beckley, and Peasmarsh. And then in October, I took part in the extremely undulating Langdale half marathon in the Lake District. This was a truly spectacular run. Starting near Sticklebarn, the route quickly arrives at Blea Tarn, where the course ascends 400ft in ½ a mile! Further along the route and stunning views of Little Langdale Tarn and the Langdale Pikes can be seen. The scenery was breathtaking, but the company was even better. I had the pleasure of running in the company of my incredibly good friend Dan, making for a magnificent and memorable experience. What a way to end a wonderful year. 2019 had been an epic and unforgettable one!

CHAPTER 14

HASTINGS PARKRUN,

NEW YEAR'S DAY, 2020

As we approached the last few months of 2019, I had the grand idea of adding a little jeopardy to my running. I'm not a big fan of short, fast races. Speed doesn't come naturally to me, and it all sounds like a lot of hard work! But, over the last few years, I'd started to reach a reasonable level of fitness, and maybe if I tweaked my training here and there, I might have a chance of setting a new 5km personal best. I hadn't run a 5-kilometre race in anger for some years, and my PB of 17:54 was set in 2012. I've always harboured an ambition to run a race time that would be good enough for an 80% - or national standard – age grading. Now, please don't think for one minute that means I would suddenly be capable of representing Great Britain – far from it! Essentially, an 80% age grading means that I'd be within 20% of the World record at a set distance for a man of my age. I hope that makes sense. I usually run within the 70% - or county standard – bracket, so to have an 80% grading – just once – would mean a great deal to me. Knowing that I'm not good enough to achieve this standard over a longer distance race, if I were to accomplish this aim, it would have to be over 5km, or not at all.

WHAT IF?

The changes in training centred around my faster sessions for the most part. Meaning that during my speed sessions, I would complete fewer repetitions, over a shorter distance, at a faster pace. And while running my tempo session, again, it would be a faster speed over a shorter distance. There were one or two variations, but essentially – throughout November and December, these sessions became part of my weekly running program, and mighty hard work they were too. As the weeks passed by, I started to see some improvement, and by the turn of the year, it was time to put all of that training into a practice race.

That practice race came in the guise of my local parkrun in good old Hastings. I'm sure most of us know what a parkrun is, but for those that don't, it is a measured 5km run that takes place all over the United Kingdom and indeed the world, at 9 am every Saturday morning. It's free to participate, and it's awesome fun! Folk complete the distance by walking, jogging, running, or combining all three. Buggies are pushed with babies spending the 3.1 miles fast asleep, children run alongside Mum, Dad, or both. Some people are using the run as part of their regular training regime, while others are covering a distance that seemed impossible only a few months ago. Runners greet people that were acquaintances just a few weeks previously, but a chance conversation that started before, during, or after a parkrun run meant that acquaintance has now become a friend. Parkrun amounts to smiles, laughs, and a wonderful sense of comradeship, and I think it has been a running revelation. The Hastings edition of this event is run along our seafront promenade, and it's an out-and-back course, starting and finishing in the same place. If it isn't a windy day (and that is rarely the case!), it's an extremely fast course.

The 1st of January 2020 arrived, and guess what? There was hardly a breath of wind in the air. Coupled with overcast skies and a cool temperature, this made for ideal conditions to establish whether or not the faster training runs were making a difference to my outright speed. As I mentioned previously, my 5km personal best stood at 17:54. If I were to get close to replicating that, I'd need to run at 5:46 per mile (or 3:35 per kilometre). I'd been able to run at this pace while doing 1-mile repeats, but I'd had a recovery jog after each rep. Up to now, I hadn't tried running at this speed beyond 1 mile at a time. My plan for today was to set off at this tempo and see how long I could sustain it for – two miles would represent real progress, and I'd know I was heading in the right direction.

I ran a very gentle two-mile warm-up before the race (my aging joints and muscles need at least that these days), and then I took my place at the start. As the starter shouted "go," I was off at what felt like unabated speed to me. No longer accustomed to racing at these ridiculous rates, this felt insanely quick. I must've looked like one of those cartoon characters when they start to run, and their legs spin like a cyclone! "This is why (pause for a breath) I hate 5k's!" I said to myself. Whereas in a half marathon or something, one can start a little slower and build into the run, that isn't possible when attempting a fast 5km. By their very definition, 5-kilometre races are short, sharp, and fast, and 1km in, I'm already breathing heavily. This was madness; I should've stayed in bed! Two kilometres covered, and the initial manic breathing is beginning to settle. I'm tucked in, alongside a local runner whom I know very well. He is fast over 5km, and so far, I've been able to stay with him – this is good. Approaching the tight turn-around cone placed at the furthest part of the course - I think "turn in wide, go through the corner and wide out. DO NOT let this tight corner break your rhythm." Exiting the 180-degree bend, I quickly get back up to speed. I've reached the turn at bang on 17:50 pace. "Come on, Ash!" I say under my breath. "Stay strong."

Shortly into the return leg, and I find myself passing the man I'd been running with. How on earth am I doing this? Something has to break soon; I can't keep up this unrelenting speed for much longer.

3k completed and my breathing is quickening now; the fast tempo is starting to have an effect. But I'm well over half distance and still on for a potential PB. 4km – my chest aches, I can't take in enough air, my heart is thumping against my rib cage, and I feel like I'm running through treacle. And my legs, oh man! My legs are aching like they have never ached before. I'm pushing my body to a new place, an uncomfortable, unfamiliar place, and yet it is responding to my every command. I can see the finish now – I look up and focus on it as hard as I can. Time to think of nothing but reaching the end. Forget the pain and discomfort; that is just a moment. Within 200 metres of the end and I dare not look at my watch; there is no comfort to be found by doing that, just keep running. I sprint the last 20 metres into the finish, and as I cross the line, the timekeeper shouts – as casually as you like – "17:40, Ash."

17:40 and a negatively split!! And on New Year's Day! This sounds like the script of a romantic, running novel. Standing there, leaning against the railings on the edge of the promenade, I can't quite believe what has just happened. Today was supposed to be a dress rehearsal and instead, it's turned out to be the main performance. Surprised, elated, and feeling slightly sick, I'm thrilled to bits, but so glad this is all over, and I NEVER want to do that again. The icing on the cake arrived with the official results. I had just scored an 81.51% age grading. This was a massive achievement for me, up there with any of my longer race personal bests. Though I'll probably never reach these dizzy heights again, I can always say that I once completed a race at a national age grading standard. Job Done!

In February, Jane and I took a short trip over to Paris. We were there to see the France v England, 6 Nations Rugby match (England lost!) but while we were there, I thought I'd indulge in a running tour around the beautiful city of lights. My 13-mile, rainy route took in Montmartre, the Paris Opera House, The Louvre, Champs-Elysees, Arc De Triomphe, the Eiffel Tower, and Notre-dame Cathedral. I started running at 6:30 am and aside from the bin men, Paris felt like it belonged to me. I love early morning, city runs, and I reckon it's a great way of seeing the highlights of a new metropolis. After a whistle-stop tour of gay Paris, Jane and I headed for a brief stay in Edinburgh, via the overnight sleeper train from London. Travelling overnight on a train was a bucket list thing for both of us and we savoured the whole experience. Ok, it wasn't quite the Orient Express, but beggars can't be choosers, right? And as far as I know, nobody was murdered, and I spotted no Belgian detectives! While enjoying the fabulous city of Edinburgh, I embarked on another, break of dawn, city run. This time, discovering the magnificent delights of the Royal Mile, Edinburgh Castle, Greyfriars Bobby, Carlton Hill, The Royal Yacht Britannia, and the 250 metre (823ft) climb up to Arthur's seat. The views across Edinburgh are spectacular from this majestic vantage point and it was well worth the climb. I really do recommend packing your running gear whenever you go on your holidays; it's a great way of doing a bit of sightseeing. We returned home and I felt refreshed and ready to continue training for the year to come, unaware that the world as we know it, was about to be thrown into turmoil.

WHAT IF?

Me just prior to the 2016 London Marathon. I'd let me training slide, and I wasn't in great shape! Photo credit Sue Martlew

Hastings Half marathon 2014. Though the responsibility weighed heavily, this was so much fun! Photo credit Unknown

WHAT IF?

*Breaking 3 hours for the first time at the Brighton marathon 2018.
My overwhelming emotion was one of relief. Photo credit Brighton marathon*

The photo of rugby legend Lewis Moody, the rugby world cup, and me wearing the white glove! Photo credit Jane Varley

*The obligatory photo with Durdle Door on the Jurassic Coast Challenge 2018.
Photo credit Jane Varley*

*The end of the South Downs Way 100 2019. My first one hundred mile finish!
Photo credit Stuart March Photography*

Even on my Honeymoon, the training didn't stop! Photo credit Jane Varley.

WHAT IF?

On my way to a ludicrous 2nd place at the North Downs Way 100 2020. Photo credit Stuart March Photography

The beautiful view from the top of Yr Wyddfa (Snowdon) in the early hours of the morning on the Snowdon24. Photo Credit Ashley Varley

*At the foot of yet another Alpine mountain on the 2022 CCC.
Photo credit UTMB*

The closing stages on the London Marathon 2022, leaving nothing out there! Photo credit London Marathon

Clutching the 2023 Male Champion trophy from the Chiltern Wonderland 50. What just happened!? Photo credit Jane Varley

The final lap of the 2023, Self Transcendence 24h Track Race. The hardest, most rewarding race I've ever run. Photo credit Jane Varley

The dream team at the end of the 2023, SDW100. Dan, Jane, me, and Lucy. Like so many others, I owe them so much. Photo credit Peter Graves

CHAPTER 15

NORTH DOWNS WAY 100, AUGUST 2020

Long before taking on the challenge of the North Downs Way 100, I was supposed to be pacing the 1-hour 40-minute group at the Hastings half marathon, which would take place in late March. This was to be followed by my 9th London Marathon in April. But with the arrival of the Covid-19 pandemic, that wasn't to be. I'd very much been looking forward to being a pacemaker at the Hastings half, and full of a sense of pride at the prospect of this amazing honour. Being a veteran of some thirteen Hastings half marathons, to be given the responsibility of leading a pace group at this historic race was very humbling. To say I was disappointed is an understatement. But given the aggressive and life-threatening nature of the coronavirus, cancelling the race was absolutely the right thing to do. Now is not the time to dwell on the pandemic; I think we've all had enough of it. The loss of life and impact on the lives of everyone has been devastating physically, fiscally, and mentally, and the repercussions of Covid-19 will be felt for many years to come and for some people, forever. On a personal level, if I considered running to be an important part of my life before the pandemic, now, it'd become vital. It turned out to be a point of focus, a familiar and much-needed friend, and a remedy to all of the stresses brought on by the virus. For me, not for the first time in my life, running was the answer.

With no races taking place in the early months of 2020, I found myself left with a somewhat elongated training period. This proved quite challenging, not least because for me a race breaks up the monotony of continual training. At times, the repetitive nature of constant training can start to feel like a treadmill that I can't get off. The best thing I could do was to find a way of altering my usual running routine so that I didn't begin to stagnate. With that in mind, I started to run on the beautiful undulations of the South Downs. Its magnificent scenery and views making for some thoroughly enjoyable and picturesque runs. I also opted to use this extra time to recce the second half of the North Downs Way 100-mile race that I would soon be doing. Knowing the parts of the course where I'd be running through the night-time darkness while feeling fatigued could only be a positive thing. As well as this, I'd added more back-to-back runs to my training regime. These runs were tough but ultimately extremely rewarding. Running, for example, 25 miles on Saturday and then 16 on Sunday was physically exhausting. However, the really tough part was raising myself mentally to get up and run on Sunday morning, following a long run the day before. These difficult, challenging weekends were a huge learning experience for me. Back-to-back runs are not just about preparing yourself physically; it's also about teaching yourself to become mentally stronger. If I could get up and do that second long run, knowing that there would be no aid stations on the route, no support, no medal, and no glory at the end of it, then hopefully, I'd be able to keep running when all of these factors applied. For my mind, this was a wonderful and important lesson and a real eureka moment that would prove most useful during the many low points of the subsequent races that I ran.

In the last week of May 2020, the wonderful folk at Centurion Running presented us all with a real, running lifeline. They had the inspired idea of organizing a race that took place over the course of one week, that participants could complete from home. To be known as the Centurion Running One Community Event, the race would consist of distances from 5km up to 100 miles, and those taking part could complete their chosen race distance in one or several runs during the course of the race week. This genius idea attracted nearly 4000 entrants, from 40 countries with runners aged from under one year old up to 86 years old. If there was ever a time when we all needed to feel part of something, to feel part of a community, that time was now. Via the wonder of social media, runners could post updates containing photos and details of their race progress, both proving to be heartening and inspiring. For one glorious week, we weren't alone. This race brought together friends and running mates who'd found themselves distanced from each other. Families pulled on their running shoes and enjoyed the great outdoors as one. The results didn't matter; that we were all out there, defying this awful virus was all that mattered. The week turned out to be a wonderful success, and Centurion Running would go on to run two similar events, later in the same year.

I'd opted for the 100-mile distance, and as part of that, I ran the 1066 Country Walk. This is a historic path that runs from Pevensey, East Sussex to the Cinque Ports town of Rye. In 1066 William, Duke of Normandy, landed his army in Pevensey and defeated King Harold in The Battle of Hastings. This 31-mile route allegedly follows the footsteps of the Norman invaders. All I know is that on a beautiful, sunny day in late May, it was a lovely path to explore, making for a memorable and rewarding run.

Running every mile of my training with the knowledge that the North Downs Way 100 might not go ahead was hard. Indeed, because of the pandemic, many of the races which Centurion Running had planned for 2020 were already postponed. Knowing this might also be the fate of the NDW100 cast a bit of shadow over my preparations. Here I was, toiling away, more committed to the task in hand than ever and yet, in the end, it may all be for nothing. However, the choices in front of me were all mine. I could either carry on training and be ready if the race took place, or step back, knowing that if the race were to happen, I would be completely unprepared. Fortunately, I made the right decision and decided on the former. Because after much hard work and I suspect many sleepless nights, Centurion Running managed to put in place Covid-19 secure measures with which they felt able to stage a safe and socially distanced race. More importantly, this meant that they were able to placate the concerns of the various organizations and agencies that they were dealing with, and all parties agreed that the race could go ahead. Great job Centurion Running!

Hopefully, I'm not the only person who has the awful habit of continually checking the weather forecast for days in the lead-up to a race. It's a daft thing to do, and in the end, the only thing this achieves is to raise my anxiety levels. The forecast leading up to the NDW100 was no exception, and as the days rolled on, the weather forecast was predicting hotter and hotter conditions for race day. Now anyone who knows me will tell you that I don't do heat. In fact, when the temperature gets above around 22 Celsius, I find just standing outside to be an uncomfortable chore! So, when 24 hours before race day, the forecast was predicting 32c, I was terrified! Though when Jane and I arrived in Farnham the evening before the race, it wasn't the temperature that concerned me, it was the humidity. Walking around Farnham town that evening, the atmosphere was so close it was ridiculous. It was insanely muggy, and just walking around the town centre left me sweating. Jane and I were sat in a restaurant having a pre-race pasta meal when I said to her, "if it's this bad in the morning, I don't think I'll be able to complete the race" I truly meant it too. I couldn't envisage for a single minute making it to the end of the 100 miles in these conditions. We got back to our small, hot, and humid hotel room, and I got into bed that night feeling thoroughly defeated and dejected – and the race hadn't even begun.

After hardly any sleep, my alarm began to ring at 4:30 in the morning. Throwing open the curtains, I discovered it was still pitch black outside. Though Jane was with me and chatting away, I was alone with my negative thoughts. Nervously contemplating the run, I got ready, had some breakfast, and anxiously made my way downstairs, preparing myself for the worst. Stepping outside for the first time that morning was a pleasant surprise. Though it was still dark, the humidity of the previous evening had fallen dramatically. It was far from comfortable, but walking to the car, I was no longer sweating. As you might imagine, this was fantastic and heartening news. If luck were really on my side, once the dawn broke, hopefully, the sun wouldn't be shining too brightly. A few wispy clouds and a gentle breeze would be just about perfect.

There was to be no mass start at this race. In normal times, people arrive at the start line and mill around chatting nervously with each other, discussing how their training had gone and what their hopes for today's race were. Then, everyone comes together for a quick briefing before setting off as one. But these were not normal times, far from it, in fact. We were in the grip of a pandemic, and one of the Covid-19 secure protocols that Centurion Running had put in place involved runners arriving and having a temperature check to ensure they weren't indicating any signs of a fever. Once this was completed, assuming no fever had been found, you were on your way. Personally, I quite liked this new way of working because I never enjoy the final hour leading up to the race start. Rocking up and running suited me perfectly and after months of training and uncertainty, my NDW100 adventure had begun!

Expecting the temperature to rise significantly during the day, I planned to start slowly. My first mile took me a steady and very pleasing 11 minutes to complete - perfect. At this stage of the day, it wasn't too hot, and as dawn broke, it was pleasing to be running in slightly overcast conditions. After the anxiety and humidity of yesterday evening, things were looking up. The first few miles drifted by, and I soon reached the small village of Puttenham. Usually, the first aid station of the race is located in this pretty village, but not this year. Because the race was to be socially distanced, the organisers were concerned that an aid station only 6 miles into the race might lead to queues of runners waiting to be fed and watered. With that in mind, it was decided to forego this checkpoint.

Jane was crewing for me once again at this race, and given the expected high temperatures, I was lucky to have her with me. A support crew essentially means that you can supplement the aid stations that are provided by the race organisers, and when the race conditions are testing, a crew really does come into its own. Immediately after crossing the River Wey, Jane and I met in Shalford Park, near Guildford. We are becoming well-practiced at this crew/racer thing now and upon my arrival, Jane changes my water bottles for two that she has already filled, and she also has with her a box filled with food for me to choose from. I've said it before, and I'll say it again Jane is THE best race crew in the world!

Shortly after Shalford Park, begins the first major climb of the day. It's quite a tough ascent and at times, the ground underfoot consists of fairly deep sandy soil. However, there is a wonderful reward at the top of the slope in the form of the beautiful church of St Martha-on-the-Hill. It's a lovely church, and as it was still early in the morning, my fellow runners and I were treated to an unspoilt view of this magnificent house of worship. If that were not enough the views from the top of the hill are amazing. I must confess to having no idea exactly what I was viewing, but nonetheless, it was a pretty spectacular sight! You then negotiate a short descent through a small wood before the course continues towards Newlands Corner and the first aid station of the day.

When comparing today's aid stations to those in more normal times, things would be vastly different during this event. We were in a pandemic now, and social distancing and cleanliness were of paramount importance. On arrival at an aid station, participants were required to wait until the food tables were clear before a volunteer would call you forward. You had to sanitize your hands on the way into the checkpoint and then select what you needed from the pre-packaged food that was on offer. In previous Centurion races that I've completed, the volunteers on duty were more than happy to fill your drinks bottles for you, but of course, that could not happen today, and if you needed a top-up, you had to do it yourself. I think this was more of a disappointment to the volunteers than the runners – because the helpers pride themselves on being as useful as possible! When exiting the aid station, you were required to sanitize your hands once again. Though all of these protocols were new to everyone, I must congratulate each and every volunteer who was working at the NDW100. The calmness and professionalism with which they carried out these new procedures made it appear like they'd been working this way for years. Every volunteer was required to wear a mask and gloves all day and to be socially distanced from the runners, resulting in none of the usual high fives or hugs. Yet undeterred, by this, the support and encouragement exhibited by all of the volunteers were incredible and humbling throughout the entire race. The Centurion Volunteer Army were and are amazing, and they rose to the occasion yet again. Well done, guys!

Pressing onwards along the course, I was feeling good and relishing the fact that the skies were still overcast, and the sun had yet to make an appearance. The route wound its way into the picturesque Little Kings Wood, and from here, the chalk trails passed many well-preserved World War Two pillboxes. Glancing to my right, it was pretty obvious to see why these pillboxes are positioned here. The path runs along a ridge and is a wonderful vantage point with far-reaching views, perfect for spotting incoming enemy planes. A few miles further down the way, I found myself in Steers field, where Jane was waiting for me. There were quite a few crews congregating, and as they patiently awaited the arrival of their own runners, many offered kind words of encouragement as other runners passed by. The views across to Dorking from this spot were mesmerizing and enchanting, a sight to behold. Some fresh energy drink and a little snack, and I was off on my merry way once again.

A short road section took me past the imposing and stunning St Barnabas Church before a long descent through the Denbies wine estate. The sun had broken through by this point, and it was beginning to warm up. But the charming views that accompanied the downward slope were enough to take my mind off the rising temperature. As we reached the bottom of the hill, the trail levelled off before reaching Box Hill and the famous steppingstones that cross the River Mole. These stones normally provide a wonderful photo opportunity for the race photographers who snap away with their cameras as runners leap from stone to stone – but not this year. This area is a popular destination for families and couples, and during these socially distanced times, the race organisers were asked to include a slight detour to the route to avoid congestion at this beauty spot. As this was the first time, I'd run the NDW100, I was blissfully unaware of any change. All I knew was that after about ½ a mile and a lot of steep and uneven steps later, we returned to the North Downs Way. I was at about quarter distance by this point and thoroughly enjoying my day – so far, so good!

The course continued along bumpy paths, through woods and a tiny hamlet or two before reaching a very sharp, energy-sapping, climb at Colley Hill. With hands on my knees, this climb had left me slightly breathless by the time I reached the top, and I was glad to reach the summit! Whereas the South Downs Way consists of rolling hills, the North Downs Way has many steep inclines to negotiate. The overall elevation gain is less on the NDW100, but the sharp ascents make it an extremely tough challenge that, for me personally, is harder than the SDW100. Once atop Colley Hill, the track passes a memorial on Reigate Hill. This memorial remembers 9 US airmen whose B-17 plane crashed here in March 1945. The memorial consists of two oak sculptures resembling wingtips that are spaced the same distance apart as the tips of a B-17 plane. It's a striking and sobering view. The next aid station, just beyond this memorial, was a welcome sight, and they had a special treat in store for us overheating runners. Packaged in small, individual bags were three cubes of ice! This was truly heaven-sent, and I grabbed a bag, immediately tucking it into the buff around my neck. The feeling as the ice melted and the cold water ran down my back was divine.

Trundling on, the route goes through the charming village of Merstham and into St Katherine's Churchyard before I met Jane once again at Rockshaw Road crew point. The heat of the day was beginning to build now, and I was so pleased to see that Jane had some ice with her too! Taking off my buff, I soaked it in the icy cold water that Jane had in a picnic box and delighted in putting it on again. The cold sensation on my hot neck was so satisfying. Onwards once more, passing the rest of the dedicated and encouraging crews before starting to climb across an arable field that led me away from Merstham. It's here that the intense heat of the day hit me for the first time. With no tree cover, and the morning clouds having broken up by now, you were exposed to the full force of the sun's rays. Coupled with the intense warmth radiating upwards from the ground below, means that the feeling of heat is crushing. By this point, about 35 miles into the race, I felt that I was progressing nicely. Though the rising temperature was starting to become a real concern.

The heat continued to rise as the miles drifted by, and I found myself losing all sense of distance and time. I suspected it must be early afternoon by now, but I couldn't be sure. Fortunately, there were plenty of shady woodlands on the route that kept the sun off my baking head. The aid stations came and went, along with steep hills and chalk paths that reflected the light and the heat of the day back up into my face. I remember thinking, "Jeez, it's getting hot, this is almost unbearable!" As I meandered along, I came across other runners who were starting to suffer in the hot conditions. We exchanged words of support and encouragement and moaned about the bloody heat! At one point, I came across two genuine, bonafide pilgrims who were walking the entire North Downs Way (or Pilgrims Way as it is also known). They were camping overnight on the trail and had been on the go for 3 days by that point, hoping to finish the walk in 7 days or thereabouts. By now I was closing in on the midway aid station. Still feeling in reasonable shape, except for a wasp sting on my shoulder (does anyone really like wasps?!), it felt amazing to be reaching the halfway point of the race. I'd no plans to hang about here though. There was another crew stop, 4 miles from here and my amazing wife would be waiting for me there.

The next four miles, between Knockholt Pound and Otford disappeared very quickly. As I'd recced the second half of the race during my training, from this point on I knew where I was going. If I needed it, an added incentive was the knowledge that Jane would be waiting for me at Otford Railway station. Having Jane with me on these long runs is a welcome and often much-needed boost. Seeing her between the Centurion aid stations is wonderful and I always look forward to her smiling face. Here was no exception and Jane was smiling and cheering as I approached her. This is where I was going to have a complete kit change, a wipe down with some baby wipes, and a brush of my teeth. About halfway through this process, a family arrived back at their car and began to ask me about the race. Where did the race start, how far have I run and how many miles had I left to go? I happily chatted with this friendly bunch as I stood in the railway station car park in my underpants with a dripping wet towel positioned on my head. I must have looked ridiculous! After a full kit change and feeling refreshed, I headed off, full of the joys of Spring. The second half of my North Downs Way adventure had started.

WHAT IF?

It's only about 5 miles from Otford to the next checkpoint in the village of Wrotham. There are one or two steep ascents to overcome along the way, and it was while negotiating this stretch that my race took a sudden and unexpected turn. Without warning, the heat of the day caught up with me. I'd been coping with the temperatures quite well to this point, but now, it hit me and hit me hard. By the time I meet Jane in Wrotham, I was feeling deflated and exhausted. Subsequently, I learned the temperature on that day had reached a high of 33c. For someone who thinks that 19c is hot, this sort of heat was ridiculous! I sat down with an ice-cold towel on my head with my shoulders dropped and legs that now felt so heavy. Feeling sick, I had to force down some rice pudding and a banana. Jane could tell that I was suffering and feeling demoralised, and she very sweetly said, "You don't have to finish this, you know." But I wasn't ready to quit just yet. In 16 miles, I'd be enjoying the company of my pacer for the rest of the run. My job now was to make it to that point. I stood up, preparing to leave and Jane said to me, "Do you know what position you are in?" "No," I replied, "and I don't want to know." Rather taken aback by this question. "Well, you are way too far up the field!" was her reply! Back on my feet, and with 60 miles completed, I set about continuing onwards – one step at a time, slowly but surely.

Early evening had arrived by now, and I reasoned that within the next hour or two, the temperature would start to drop significantly as the sun began to set. I just needed to get through the next couple of hours, and running would become much easier. About five miles outside of Wrotham, I entered Trosley Country Park. This is a beautiful woodland, and the late evening sun piercing through the trees and lighting up the trail in front of me was beautiful. The route consisted of a lovely, gentle descent and making my way down the hill, I began to work on a few calculations. I'd surmised that with about 35 miles to go, if I could travel at 4 miles an hour, it would still be possible to finish in around 22 hours. "I can do that," I thought to myself, "that is 15 minutes per mile and if I keep that pace up, I'll be well inside my 24-hour target." Buoyed by my impressive maths skills and beginning to feel a whole lot better about life, I managed to complete the next mile in 13 minutes, and then the subsequent two miles in 24 minutes. It seemed that I've found my mojo again and my head was back in the game.

A few miles - and a tough climb up some steps - later, I'd reached the awesome gang at Holly Hill aid station. They were a cheerful bunch and keeping them company was a skeleton sat comfortably in a chair! It seemed that this runner had been sitting down here for WAY too long! Oh, and they have Battenberg cake too! Does life get any better? Bidding my new friends farewell I headed off into the fading twilight. The route traversed another lonely and remote wood that left me with an uncomfortable feeling of isolation. It was great to leave this desolate wood behind and once I'd emerged into the late evening sunshine, I could just about make out the River Medway in the distance. The River Medway crossing is probably the dullest place I'd ever run in my entire life! To cross the river, one has to follow a path that runs parallel with the M2 motorway for approximately one mile. It's noisy, smelly, and just about the most unpleasant place to run I can think of, and it was a relief to reach the end of the tarmac footpath where the racket from the cars began to fade. Following the North Downs Way back under the M2 and away from the motorway, I was overjoyed to be leaving the traffic noise behind me.

At this stage, I was now only three miles from Bluebell Hill checkpoint and the company of Paul, my pacer. The only thing that stood between me and my buddy was a long uphill rise. When I'd recced this section of the course, the climb up Bluebell Hill had been a real struggle and I ended up walking the majority of it. But today I felt determined to jog up the whole thing. How slowly I was moving mattered not one bit, just as long as I didn't walk. Looking over to my right as I ascended the hill, my eyes were fixed on another dramatic sunset. It wasn't quite as spectacular as the dusk I'd encountered on the South Downs Way 100 in 2019, but it was impressive, nonetheless. In the end, I just about made it up the slope – with a brief stop for a little breather – and cresting the hill, safe in the knowledge that the next aid station is now very close, I couldn't wait to see Jane and Paul.

I reached Paul (who had arrived with a few hours to spare this time!) and Jane, who was waiting alongside him with drinks and a box of goodies! While I tucked into my sandwiches and cocktail sausages, I could feel Paul looking at me. His eyes were carrying out a visual check to see how I looked – was I standing awkwardly, did I look uncomfortable or in pain? As we set off for the last 27 miles of the race, Paul conducted a very matter-of-fact Q&A session with me. How had my day been, how was I feeling now, and what was I hoping for from the rest of the race? Answers duly given; Paul had all the ammunition he needed to help me through the rest of the run. Paul is an ultra-running legend and one of the top dogs of pacing. I always feel lucky and eternally grateful for the knowledge and support that he brings with him. I'd need all of that expertise as we headed into one of the toughest parts of the race.

Together we continued on, over the steep descents and ascents that make up the stretch between Bluebell Hill and Detling. My quad muscles were killing me by now, the sharp downward slopes that I'd encountered during the last 76 miles having done their worst. Every downhill step was agony, and the harshest were yet to come. After another steep drop, Paul and I arrived at Detling aid station. The checkpoint is located in a village hall, but I didn't need to go in because Jane was there with everything I needed, and a very welcome hug to boot. She knew that I'd been dreading the next few miles more than any other part of the course. The steps between Detling and Hollingbourne are infamous among NDW100 veterans. I'd experienced climbing up and down these very stairs during a recce of the course, and, on that day, I was only 8 miles into my run when I arrived at them. I'd struggled then, so how would I cope with 80 miles in my legs? This I wasn't looking forward to! We began the first descent down the steep uneven steps. It was dark by now, we had our head torches on, and watching where my feet were landing had become a massive priority. This section of the route continues in the same vein for about 5 or 6 miles, and along with the treacherous steps, the path is narrow and rutted, and trees are often hanging at head height, across the trail. Ducking under them after 80-odd miles on my feet proved to be a challenge! At one point, tripping on a rock and landing on my face, I began to curse my stupidity. "Ash, it's okay," said Paul, "don't be so hard on yourself. You are tired now, just try and concentrate on picking your feet up." After what felt like an endless series of quad-killing, up and down steps, delight filled my heart as we reached the last descent into Hollingbourne village. Seeing the lights of the houses and cottages ahead of me, the sense of relief was palpable. There were about 15 miles to go from here and those miles were predominantly flat ones too!

A quick snack provided by my darling wife accompanied by smiles of relief because the worst was over, and the two of us were running again. The miles ticked by as Paul and I discussed everything and nothing, and remarkably quickly, we had reached the 91-mile checkpoint on the outskirts of Lenham. At this point, I heard a volunteer nonchalantly say to me, "You are in second place, 50 minutes behind the leader!" "Bugger off," I replied. "No seriously," was the retort. This news was as surprising as it was ridiculous. Me, a have-a-go-hero, in second place, how the hell did this happen!? Paul had said something to me a couple of hours ago about being in the top three, but I'd paid little attention, yet here was this chap, confirming Paul's words. Staggered and slightly confused, Paul and I headed off along the trail. How the heck had I ended up in second place?

My head was spinning, and suddenly I felt a strange sense of pressure that I wasn't altogether comfortable with. I'd never even contemplated what position I might finish the race in, yet here I was with the chance of a top-three finish in a 100-mile race. Armed with this knowledge, I picked up the pace. A little too quickly as it turned out because a mile or so after leaving Lenham aid station, I was really struggling. Feeling sick and aching all over, I needed to walk for a while. I'd be meeting Jane for the last time in the village of Charing, and that was only about 3 miles from where we currently were. The three miles between us seemed to take an age to complete, and as I reached Jane, I was feeling utterly depleted. The highlight of those previous three miles of hell had been nearly tripping over an owl as it took off in front of us! I'd never seen an owl in the wild before, and Paul and I didn't spot it until it was almost too late! Finally seeing Jane, after what seemed like an age, was a huge relief; I had no energy; my legs were broken and hurting like hell, and I wanted to throw up. I knew it was vital for me to eat something, or I'd never make it to the end. I forced down a banana and half a cookie and started walking slowly once more. For the last 10 miles, we'd been crisscrossing a couple who were crewing a young lad, currently lying in third position, and they were here, once again, awaiting his arrival. "How are you feeling?" one of them asked me with a cheery smile. "Battered. My quads are so sore, and I'm completely exhausted," I replied. "Bless you, keep going," she said. "Actually, you shouldn't have told us that, we'll let our runner know and he will be chasing you down!" This, I'm sure, was said in jest. But to me, it was like a red rag to a bull! It was time to stop feeling sorry for myself and run already!

Now I'll tell anyone who asks or who cares to listen that I'm not competitive. Never have been, never will be. But after hearing those words, my tired, broken body was instantly transformed! Paul and I set off on what can only be described as a progression training run, and with about 7 miles to go until the end of the race, I was running like a scared rabbit in headlights! I got faster and faster as the miles continued, only stopping briefly to check in at the final aid station in Dunn Street, 4 miles from the end. Once we got off the trails and hit the tarmac on the outskirts of Ashford, there was no stopping me. Approaching the final run into the finish, with the Julie Rose stadium and the finish line in sight, I turned to Paul and, referring to the poor devil behind me, said, "You'll have to get up much earlier in the morning if you want to catch me before the end of this race!" I must confess that I'm utterly ashamed of my bombastic words and my pomposity, and the only defense I can offer is that I was feeling punchy!

We entered the stadium concourse, and through the darkness, we found our way onto the track, sprinting around the final 300m. We'd just completed the 103rd mile (yes, this 100-mile race actually consists of 103 miles!) in under 7 minutes 30 seconds. At Bluebell Hill checkpoint, 27 miles before the finish, I'd been 50 minutes behind the race leader. Crossing the finish line, I was 13 minutes behind him. This had been one heck of a day, full of trials and tribulations and finally, I'd made it to the end in second place, earning another 100-mile - One Day -buckle in the process. Below is something I posted on social media in the aftermath of the race. I think it represents a fair and honest appraisal of my run at the NDW100.

I think I will call this post; every dog has its day!

My finish time at the 2020 North Downs Way 100 would have given me a finishing position of between approximately 10th and 20th place at the last three NDW100 races. But... somehow, this year, it was good enough for second overall!! I am no elite ultrarunner, and I have never placed anywhere near that high before - and I doubt I will again. But luck was on my side in 2020, and I will forever be able to say that once - just once - I finished in second place at a 100-mile race! When I look at the results, I still can't believe that my name is there, just behind the winner!

For me, these races are very much a team thing, and to that end, I have to thank a few people. Firstly, my beautiful wife, Jane, who was my crew for the day. Jane kept me fed and watered and gave me endless encouraging hugs! I love you, honey. My incredible pacer,

Paul McCleery, who joined me at Bluebell Hill. He got me through the Detling Hills, and when I was flagging around Charing, he kept me moving until I found the inner strength to push on to the end. Paul is so much more than a pacer; he is an inspiration and a great friend. And of course, the amazing Centurion volunteers. As ever, you were all friendly, encouraging, kind, thoughtful, and full of cheers and smiles. You were the Guinea Pigs for a new way of doing things this year, and you did it like you had been doing it for years. Thank you all so much.

I have been running for about 15 years now, and I've reached the ripe old age of 48! During the last three years, I have worked hard on improving and maximizing my training. The result has been new personal bests from 5k up to the marathon distance, and I have discovered the brilliance of ultra-running. And with a bit of luck, I managed a result at the NDW100 that was beyond my wildest dreams! The only advice I can offer is, work hard, believe in yourself, and never stop dreaming. You never know what you might achieve! I mean - this dog has had its day!

CHAPTER 16

LONDON MARATHON OCTOBER 2020

I was supposed to run the London Marathon in April 2020 along with nearly 40,000 other eager runners. Memories should have been made, and new friendships formed as we ran around the streets of one of the great capital cities of the world. But sadly, the uncompromising acceleration of the Covid-19 pandemic meant that the London Marathon, along with the majority of spring races in 2020, fell victim to the virus. This was entirely understandable and the right thing to do given the circumstances, but that doesn't mean the sense of disappointment was any less real for everyone involved. The plan initially was to move the race to October 2020 when it was hoped the pandemic would be under control, and we could have a real party atmosphere at the race. However, as the seriousness of the disease began to sink in, it was inevitable that the race would have to be cancelled. Places would be deferred to subsequent years, and one glorious day, every single 2020 entrant would be given the opportunity to run their London Marathon. But what to do about London 2020? In the end, the organisers came up with a brilliant plan that would involve runners taking part in their own socially distanced marathons. Each runner would complete their individual race around the streets, lanes, and trails of towns, cities, and villages all over the world. Even though the pandemic was keeping us apart, we would come together in an act of defiance and say to this virus, you may alter where we run, you may stop us running en masse, but you will never stop us running. Humanity was the clear winner as millions of pounds were raised for many worthwhile charities that were struggling for survival in the current environment. How we deal with adversity is part of what defines us, and this show of strength felt like a real kick in the teeth for this virus!

I live in Hastings, East Sussex, but I'd grown up in Lowestoft, Suffolk – the most easterly point of England. Though born in Hastings, when I was just a toddler, my parents separated, and I ended up moving with Mum to a new part of the country. Eventually, I would return to the town of my birth, aged nineteen. Packing my belongings into my battered red Fiesta, I headed south and back to 1066 country. I hadn't returned to Lowestoft for over 25 years, and Jane had always been curious about the town where I'd lived as a boy. So, we formulated a plan and decided that we'd make this unique London Marathon even more special and spend a weekend exploring the town where I grew up. On the Sunday morning, when the marathon would take place, I came up with a route that would incorporate the houses, schools, workplaces, and haunts of my youth. This was going to be a real trip down memory lane, assuming I could still find my way around Lowestoft all these years on!

I set the alarm to go off nice and early on Sunday morning, and, amid much excitement, I rose out of bed and threw open the curtains only to discover it was chucking it down! It was still dark, and the streetlights were lighting up the puddles that had been formed by the heavy rain. It would be fairly accurate to say that these were not exactly the conditions I'd been hoping for! The whizz kids at the London Marathon had developed an app that would track your progress while you ran and then automatically stop once you'd completed the marathon distance. Technology is alien to me, but I'd at least managed to download the app to my phone successfully. I left the hotel we were staying at, hit the start button on the app, and just like that, my race had begun! The trip down memory lane route that I'd planned was a little short of the requisite 26.2 miles, so my cunning plan was to add a couple of loops here and there to make up the shortfall. I wasn't thinking about that right now, though; the only thing on my mind was my nostalgic run, which was underway and filling me with exciting and nervous anticipation!

I didn't have to go far before passing a fish shop, located near the docks, where I'd worked during weekends as a teenager. Honestly, it wasn't the best job in the world, but it did pay more than my previous, floor cleaning job, at a local minimarket. The real downside was that I regularly stunk of fish, creating a rather unwanted problem! When you're a fifteen-year boy, beginning to show an interest in the opposite sex, this fishy aroma is far from ideal! When I was growing up, Lowestoft had a thriving offshore fishing industry. Trawlers would regularly spend around two weeks at sea before returning to the market with their catch. Back then, it seemed that every family had links to fishing via direct employment or working for businesses that supported and serviced the fishing industry. I learned on my return to Lowestoft that the fishing had all but gone now. I don't fully understand why, but I do know that it made me feel a little sad. But, on with the run, and a few hundred metres from the shop where I developed my noxious stench is a road bridge that separates one side of the docks from the other. The bridge carries a major trunk road in and out of Lowestoft, and it's been known to get stuck open on more than one occasion, often resulting in major traffic chaos. As I approached, as if welcoming a returning son, the bridge began to open, right on cue. In its way, it's quite a regal sight, and it was great and somewhat fitting to witness it once again. A few miles later I found myself passing one of the primary schools that I'd attended and the workshops of Beeline Refrigeration, with whom I'd started my engineering apprenticeship. It was around this point it dawned on me that I hadn't heard anything from the app. Not that I was particularly expecting anything, you understand, but as I was listening to music through my earphones, I thought that maybe I might get an update on my progress or something. My watch had recorded nearly seven miles by now, but not a sound or vibration from the app had appeared on my phone. "Best check," I thought.

DISASTER! Taking my phone from my pocket, what did my eyes see staring back at me? The same screen that I'd last looked at when leaving my hotel lobby. The bloody thing hadn't started! I couldn't have pressed the start button properly. What a plonker, as they say in Peckham! Why the hell hadn't I double-checked? Seven miles in, and the app had recorded zilch! Panic set in as I began to contemplate what to do next. "Well hitting the damn start button might be quite a good idea!" I chastised myself! That done (definitely this time!), I began to run again and wondered what to do next. Should I phone Jane to see if she could do a bit of research for me and find out what to do if the app hadn't started? Or do I stop and search for that information on the app myself - there must be a Q and A on here. In the end, I decided to start running again and keep on running. This was my cock-up after all! Another mile down the road and suddenly my music is interrupted by the sound of Steve Cram's voice as he congratulates me on completing my first mile. "I'm nearly 8 miles in mate!" I replied to this pre-recorded voice, like I was expecting Steve to apologise or something!

My extended marathon continued, and my route took me past homes and schools that made up much of my childhood. Distant memories were brought to mind of friends and teachers who had played a part in my formative years. As I ran around the streets of Lowestoft, new roads appeared and out-of-town shopping complexes that hadn't existed when I lived in the town. They were a reminder of how the towns and cities where we live have evolved and changed over the past quarter-century. I was wearing the race number that the London Marathon had sent me in my race pack (it seemed the right thing to do), and noticing a couple of runners looming into view, I could see that they were wearing London numbers too. Strangely, I hadn't expected this and as the rain came down and the wind blew a chilly breeze, it was heart-warming to see other London Marathon participants running towards me. In this weird, socially distanced world in which we currently live, we exchanged cheers and thumbs up by way of encouragement and went our separate ways. On more than one occasion, during my run, passing motorists saw me and tooted their horns and cheered. This was turning into an unexpectedly emotional experience! Approaching the marathon distance, I realised I still had a chance of registering a time of under 3 hours 10 minutes (on my watch, that is, which I'd definitely started leaving the hotel!) and instinctively my pace increased. In the end, my watch recorded the 26.2 miles, in just over 3:09. Almost simultaneously Paula Radcliffe's voice, accompanied by cheers and claps emanated from the app, congratulating me on reaching 19 miles! Why hadn't I double-checked the app when I left the hotel!? Because I'd accelerated to get under 3:10, I was now suffering, and I still needed to run nearly 7 miles to record an official finish on the London Marathon app! The rest of the run was quite a struggle and approaching my hotel, with only 1 mile to go, the music I'd been listening to, abruptly stopped. Had my earphones run out of charge? Or was it – "Oh no don't be the phone!" I thought! Sure enough, my phone battery had died, and the phone switched itself off!

Back at our hotel room, I plugged my phone into its charger, switched it on, and nervously opened the marathon app. Much to my relief, it'd automatically paused my run and I only needed to run another ½ a mile to reach the finish. With a bit of life in my phone battery, I set off once again and at long last, I completed the race. Feeling utterly exhausted, I was revelling in the sound of Mr. Cram congratulating me for finishing when once more, the sound of silence filled my ears. Yet again, my useless phone had expired! At least I'd recorded an official finish – and just in the nick of time! In the end, I ran just over 33 miles, and it turned out that I could've submitted the time and distance from my watch to the London Marathon website after all. But I really wanted to see that finish time on the app, even if it meant running an ultramarathon! Oh, and guess what? Along with my fellow 37,965 virtual London Marathon finishers, I'm now a Guinness World Record holder! Yes, folks, all of us who finished the race hold the record for the "Most users to run a remote marathon in 24 hours." And I have the certificate to prove it!

Ok, I've thought long and hard about including what you're about to read next and writing these words, I'm feeling nervous, anxious, and very exposed. This is because I never want anyone to view the Ashley they know today any differently because of the following words. If that's you, please don't do that. The thing is, there was a greater, more personal reason for my returning to Lowestoft that only I knew about. This little town holds memories that haunt me to this day, and I hoped my return and my run would exorcise a few demons. I was about to find out.

Whilst growing up in Lowestoft, I was subjected to abuse at the hands of my stepfather. I'm not ready to go into graphic detail here, and there's nothing to be gained by doing that. What I will say is that I was subjected to disgusting and vile behaviour that no child should ever experience. The abuse took place at one address, and as part of my route, I'd decided to run straight past that house. Approaching it, my heart was beating fast, and I felt incredibly uneasy. As the moment of truth arrived, with my heart racing, I stood as tall as possible, stuck out my chest and held my head high and, in an act of conscious defiance, I ran strong with my eyes fixed on the house. Passing what had once felt like a prison to me, I was thinking, "Look at me now, this is who I am, and you did not break me."

Now, at last, perhaps we come to the real reason why running has become so important to me. It's not about personal bests or medals – every run feels like a small victory for me because when I lace up my trainers, each mile run distances me further from a past that brought me much pain and sadness. But on this day, running past this home from long ago, I was no longer running away from my past – a scared and frightened little boy – I was running straight towards it – a man who refuses to be caged by my history.

To this day, I carry the scars formed during those dark days, months, and years. They aren't physical, you understand; they are emotional, and they manifest themselves in various ways, including shyness and a lack of self-confidence. I disguise these traits extremely well, though I know they'll forever be a part of me. Often, I prefer to be alone because life is easier and safer that way; I have little or no self-belief and real issues with trust. Child abuse, whether it be physical or emotional, through neglect, hunger, or any other reason is wrong, and it causes damage that often lasts a lifetime. As humans, as a society, and as a global civilization, we must do all that we can to eradicate this from our world.

All of this begs the question, why write about it? Well, I wish for my story to be a message of hope and optimism. As I've already said, though living with wounds that will never heal, I refuse to live in a prison created by someone else. Allowing those walls to confine me means giving up on life and on myself. Very often, I encounter situations and events that make me feel vulnerable and uncomfortable, and I work hard to rise above them. There is a real duality to my personality. Ash, the runner, is more confident and comfortable in others' company. Get me talking about running, and I won't shut up! Away from running, I can be awkward and aloof. I wish that weren't the case, but sadly, it is. Over the years, running has empowered me, and through it and because of it, I've gained more confidence. The personal triumphs I've attained help develop an inner belief that permeates into the rest of my life. It's no exaggeration to say that running has been my salvation.

I'm not naive enough to think this could help everyone, or indeed that everyone can be helped. We are all individuals, and we deal with trauma and suffering in our own, often unique ways. There are many who never come to terms with abuse, and the suffering it causes can last a lifetime. It is important that we recognize and understand that. Anyone who suffers abuse during childhood is a victim of neglect and circumstances that they never created, and many suffer in silence. I'm one of the lucky people who've been able to develop a coping mechanism. These days, I've reconciled with my past. Though I have weak moments, I'm resolute and determined in my efforts to rise above adversity with pride and dignity. For me, this represents the greatest success of them all. In Jane, I have a fantastic wife who brings peace and contentment to my world in a way I never imagined possible. What I do know is that it's the most fantastic feeling. I have two beautiful children, and it'll be a privilege and a joy to watch them grow and develop – who knows, maybe grandchildren one day! I think it was Martin Luther King Jr who once said, "Only when it's dark enough can you see the stars." Jane and my daughters are those stars, and they shine so brightly, leaving me feeling like the luckiest man alive.

CHAPTER 17

THE END?

So, we've finally arrived at what would be the toughest running challenge of my life. I'd been contemplating and considering entering this since I ran my first 100-mile race in 2019, and I'd finally made up my mind. This was the year that I would attempt the Centurion Running Grand Slam – four 100-mile races in one year. This was my shot at the big one, and as the dawn broke on 2021, I was full of excitement, trepidation, and nervous anticipation. I'd entered all the races, and my place on the starting line was secure. The right preparation was all that was needed, and if I'd thought that training for one ultra-distance race was hard enough, this was going to be on a wholly different level. I knew that and felt it intensely.

Training began in a sort of funk that is normally associated with the post-Christmas period. Sort of stuttering and sluggish, coupled with being a few pounds heavier than I had been a couple of weeks ago, before the festivities began! This was not the year to overindulge during the Christmas period, but as I seem to do every year, overindulge I did! However, training had started reasonably well, and when I set off for an easy-paced 10-mile run on a cold, crisp but beautifully sunny morning in early January, I was full of optimism. Everything was progressing perfectly normally, and I was enjoying the fresh, winter air, and the warm sunshine when I started to feel a niggling pain in the back of my right calf. As we runners normally do, initially, I thought it was just a normal running ache, which would wear off in due course, so I just trudged on, trying not to think about it. However, that niggling pain began to become a constant ache, pulling at the back of my leg, and reminding me with every step that it was there and wasn't about to go away. After a couple of miles, the inevitable happened, and I had no choice but to stop and begin the slow walk back home. All the way back, my mind was racing. "Was this it? Was the dream over before it had even started?" By the time I'd reached my front door, the panic that had been building inside of me had begun to subside a little. I would go indoors, get some ice on the troubled muscle, and take a few days off. It wasn't that painful, so no need for melodrama, histrionics, and alarming thoughts. However, 10 days later, despite plenty of R.I.C.E (rest, ice, compression, and elevation), that ache was still there, and running on it was proving to be impossible. I could walk ok, but try and even jog, and the pain and tightness were still there. This meant only one thing, I was going to have to face my fears and set up the dreaded turbo trainer! Now, I love running; it's become a part of me, but running on a treadmill – I just can't stand it. Running and going nowhere, staying in the same place, looking at the same view, and listening to that constant, mind-numbing whirring drives me insane. It works for many people, but not for me. But this pales into insignificance when compared to sitting on a bike, fitted to a turbo trainer, endlessly pedalling on the spot. Every second feels like a minute, every minute like an hour and so on. It's a form of torture that I have nightmares about. But I needed to keep up my cardiovascular training without putting any load on my sore muscle. So, if this is what it was going to take, then this is what I was willing to do to keep my grand slam dream alive!

And so I began this very alien and unfamiliar training routine, which involved strength training twice a week (without aggravating my poorly calf), sitting on my static bike three times a week, in our sweaty conservatory pedalling like a fury (whilst trying to think of anything other than pedalling like a fury), then at the weekends, I would hop on my bike and go and do battle with the traffic and the Lycra-clad proper cyclists for three or four hours. I would often find myself engulfed by a swiftly moving peloton consisting of genuine cyclists, on their very expensive carbon-framed bikes who must've wondered what this mobile roadblock, dressed in running clothes and riding an aging commuter bike was doing on the road. Come to think of it, I often found myself thinking the very same thing as I negotiated yet another pothole, cursing the cold winter weather that was chilling me to the bone. This was not fun, but at least I was outside. Anything was better than that darn turbo trainer! Then once every two weeks, I'd cross my fingers, pray to any God or deity that might be listening, and attempt to go for a gentle run. But alas, every time I tried, within a few minutes, my annoying calf pain would reappear. I consulted a physio who promised me that there was nothing seriously wrong with my lower right leg, and given time, I would be up and running again with gusto. The problem was, I didn't have time, and in the end, it wasn't until late March before I was able to run again. And even then, it was only for one minute of jogging followed by one minute of walking for a couple of miles. In the end, it wouldn't be until mid-April before I could run for a few miles without a walking break. With the Thames Path 100 only a matter of weeks away, despite my best efforts to maintain a degree of fitness throughout the past few months, reality hit home with an inevitable thump. The grand slam was over before it had even begun. In truth, I had known that some time ago, and I'd been clinging to a false hope.

To say I was devastated would be an understatement. The Centurion grand slam was supposed to be the glorious end to this journey. One huge crescendo at the end of it all, the icing on the cake, my chance to become a legend in my own lunchtime. I mean – as I said in the Preface - this was what this whole book was supposed to be about; this was supposed to be the epic conclusion to the blood, sweat, and tears of this journey. But it wasn't to be, and that hurt like hell. In truth, once I'd begun running again, it became all too obvious to me that, despite the cycling and the hiking that I'd been doing in a vain attempt to stay fit, my fitness level had dropped significantly. There was no way I was going to be able to run for 100 miles anytime soon. I was hurt, demoralised, depressed, and I just wanted to wallow in my own self-pity. Of course, all of this was happening whilst the world was gripped by the horrendous effects of the Coronavirus pandemic, which made my little problem seem wholly irrelevant. People were losing loved ones and jobs, unable to see family and friends, wondering when (and if) all of this would come to an end. This should've put my own minor problem into perspective. There would be other grand slams, and other races. I would wake up tomorrow, and my life – my beautiful life, which I'm very lucky to have – would be just the same. But I would be lying if I said that I wasn't incredibly disappointed. Whilst sitting at my computer, carrying out the unenviable task of withdrawing my grand slam race entries, I did make one important decision – There was no way this journey was about to end here, especially not in this way.

CHAPTER 18

NEW BEGINNINGS

When I said that I'd withdrawn from all the grand slam races, that isn't strictly true. By mid-April, I was back to something resembling normal training, and rebuilding my running fitness had begun. With that in mind, I'd kept my spot in the Autumn 100, which wouldn't take place until October. That meant I had plenty of time to continue to patiently build up my training, with a view to hopefully having a good run in October. By way of preparation, I entered two build-up races. The first was the 50k Weald Challenge, which took place in June. It's a beautiful route, starting and finishing in the village of Chiddingly, East Sussex, and it takes in parts of the Vanguard Way, the Ashdown Forest, and the Weald Way. The organisers are incredibly enthusiastic, and the race is worth doing, if only for the commemorative pottery mug that they hand out for completing the run. I still have my morning coffee from that very mug! The run itself took place on a very hot summer's day, and given the conditions, I was pretty pleased with 5th overall, in a time of 4 hours 40 minutes. The second race was the much bigger (and probably more fashionable) Race to the Stones in mid-July. The route starts in Lewknor, Oxfordshire, finishing in Avebury in Wiltshire, along the Ridgeway path. There are various race distances involved, and I'd opted for the 100k. Leading up to the race, training had been progressing fairly well, and as race day dawned with gorgeous sunshine, I was feeling pretty good. One of the reasons I'd opted for this race was that the 100k distance took in some of the route that I would run during the Autumn 100-mile race. So, not only would I be building much-needed confidence and fitness, but I would also be carrying out a recce of parts of the A100 as well. The race itself was uneventful until the last 15 miles or so. At that stage, I'd begun to realize that if I could maintain a reasonable pace, I had a real chance of getting under 10 hours over 100k for the first time. Challenge accepted; I began to focus on my target. The brain was willing, but by this stage, the legs, and the feet (courtesy of the relentless chalk path) were beginning to suffer, and with about 5 miles to go – and still on target (just) – the race reached a very rutted mud path. My word, did I ever curse my way along that damn path! It was so uneven, and I found myself leaping from side to side in an attempt to navigate the best route through the minefield under my feet. That all sounds like a fantastic idea until you consider that by this stage, anything other than forward motion was playing havoc with my aching legs. Lateral movement was not a smart idea, and I nearly cramped a couple of times.

The stones in question in the race name consist of the Avebury stone circle, and with a couple of miles to go, by way of a highlight of the race, you circumnavigate these magnificent stones. Now, incredible as these stones are, with 60 miles in my legs, and chasing a target that was becoming ever harder to attain by the second, I couldn't give a toss as to the history, structure, or beauty of these hunks of rock – I just wanted to see the back of them! Fortunately, they were rounded in a flash, and I was on the final push, through one more field of knee-deep – energy-sapping – grass before turning onto a concrete farm path for the final push. I could see the finish gantry, tantalizingly coming into view in the distance. I still had time, if I could just keep going. Checking my watch, I see that time is ticking away, and looking up, the finish doesn't seem to be getting any closer. I repeated this process about 50 times until – after what seemed like an eternity – I finally passed under the finish arch in a time of 9:55:42. 100k in under 10 hours – done!

The next day, Jane took part in the 50k race, and for the first time ever, it was me who took over crewing duties. If I thought that racing was tough, this was something else. I've never been so nervous at a race in my life. Waiting at each crew point for my wife to appear was stomach-churning. Having no idea of how her race was going and how she was feeling was terrible and nerve-wracking. Each time she arrived at our predetermined meeting point, she'd be smiling and happy, whilst I'd bitten my nails down to the quick, in a panic, wondering if Jane would still be walking when I saw her. This experience really opened my eyes as to how difficult being a crew for a runner can be. And yet, on the endless occasions that Jane has done it for me, she has never appeared flustered or overawed; instead, she is the picture of calm. If I ever needed it, this was a reminder of just how lucky I am. This was the first time Jane had completed an ultra-distance race, and I was so proud of her. As she crossed the finish, I had a bunch of flowers and a card waiting in my arms, along with a huge hug. It was partly to celebrate her epic achievement, but also because I wanted to let her know how much I loved her, and how proud of her I was – and am.

Talking of having a crew, there is something unique about the A100 amongst the one hundred mile Centurion races, because it's the only one where you are not allowed to be crewed. The reason for this is that the run consists of four out-and-back legs that return to a central starting position (located at the race headquarters) at the end of each leg. Each one consists of a 25-mile leg, with aid stations on route every 6 miles, and you are allowed to have a kit bag at the race HQ containing everything you may need for your run. All this means that crew are really surplus to requirements. Though I have to say, this was slightly alarming for me. Because, at the previous one hundred mile races that I'd run, all I had to think about was moving forward in the right direction. Between the excellent, Centurion aid stations, and my awesome wife, all the other logistics associated with running such a long way were taken care of for me. Food, drink, clothing, medication, you name it, someone else was taking care of it. But at this race, I was at least going to have to take care of some of my own housekeeping and wellbeing. Bearing that in mind, I'd written what I would appropriately describe as my idiot list, which I'd place on top of everything in my bag. This was a clear and concise list of things that I should not forget to do each time I returned to the race HQ. Surely even I couldn't mess that up – or so I hoped!

The race started with a persistent drizzle as my fellow runners and I gathered at Goring on Thames village hall for the first 25-mile leg, which went pretty much to plan for me. In these early stages of an ultra race, I often find myself engulfed by my fellow runners. We all have our own strategy for completing ultra distances, and mine is to try and be as consistent with my pacing throughout the race as I can be. Obviously, there are times when the topography of the route does not allow for this, but leg one of the A100 is pancake flat, meaning that even pacing is very achievable. My first visit to my kit bag at the race HQ went well (well done, Ash!), and with nothing overlooked, I set off on the slightly lumpier leg two. I knew this section very well, having completed all of it during the Race to the Stones. That meant I knew exactly where the surprisingly steep sections of the course were. But, by the end of leg two, I was feeling strong, and I'd begun to haul my way back through the field. Night fell on leg three (another part of the route I recognised from the Race to the Stones) and the long steady climbs of this portion of the race proved to be quite the challenge. The A100 was also to be the first race where I'd spend more time running through the darkness of the night than I would during the light of the day, which would be a new challenge. My previous 100-mile ultras had taken place in the summer, and we were now deep into the autumn months. Leg three proved to be a long grind, and I was glad to reach the pretty village of Goring once again. A change of clothes, some food and drink, and I was off on the final stage of the race. This leg of the route (like the first) closely follows the Thames, and with an eerie mist hanging over the water, a distinct chill in the air, and my increasing tiredness, I was having to concentrate hard on the course markers guiding my way. Nevertheless, at one point I still managed to take a wrong turn, almost ending up in the Thames! As I approached the halfway spot of this stage near Reading, I passed a bunch of well-lubricated chaps, sat around a campfire, enjoying an evening by the Thames. The warmth of the fire and the convivial atmosphere created by this group of friends were hard to resist. Of course, this is an out and back leg, and if I thought it'd been hard to pass this motley crew first time around, it was nigh impossible to ignore on the second occasion! But I fought the urge manfully, and with a knee that was becoming increasingly painful, I staggered my way to the end of what had been an awesome run in a new personal best of 17:13:49. Following what had been a very difficult start to the year, where my dreams had been shattered, this felt fantastic. My third one-hundred miler was in the bag, and I'd even managed to crew myself! I gave myself a well-earned pat on the back and made my contented way home.

As well as the four stages that make this race distinctive among Centurion 100s, there is also another unique element. The out-and-back nature of the race means that we get the rare opportunity to see all our fellow runners during the run. For me, this was a real highlight of the race. From the guys who are leading the way to my fellow racers who are further down the field, everybody is being the very best that he or she can be – giving it their all and facing the difficult challenge head-on. It's humbling and beautiful and something I would be lucky enough to experience once again in the future. Each and every one of them exchanged words of support and encouragement with me as we pursued our common goal of making it to the end. Ultra racing really is a unique and special thing.

WHAT IF?

The A100 brought to an end a run of three races in four weekends. The others were another 26.2-mile tour around the historic streets of London, and the Goodwood marathon, where I secured another Good for Age London Marathon qualifying time. The Goodwood race represents a great opportunity for Good for Age qualification. This is because the tarmac is smooth, there are no tight turns, and if you can get your head around the monotony of 11 laps of the grand prix circuit, it really is a fast course.

With another leg of my running journey completed, thoughts shifted towards 2022, and I had a secret that only I knew about. A secret that would take me higher than I had ever been before.

CHAPTER 19

GOING UP!

My 2022 racing year began in a car park in Wendover, Buckinghamshire, in early January. The car park of the Shoulder of Mutton pub, to be precise. On a cold, wet January day, this was the start location for the 43-mile Country to Capital race. Starting from here, the route passed through the beautiful countryside of Buckinghamshire before joining the Grand Union Canal for the final 15 miles or so. The winter of '21/22 had been wet, very wet! I mean, even wetter than a really wet thing! That made for some treacherous conditions underfoot as we made our way across the trails and farmland of leafy Buckinghamshire, and the puddles on the canal towpath were like miniature ponds! The rain was unrelenting for the whole race, and I can tell you I wasn't having fun. But it was a good test of my mental resilience (I think they call it character building!), and it showed that what had been a tough winter of training had been worth it. Winter training miles are not my favourite thing, and I have to dig really deep to get myself out in the wind and the rain. Needless to say, when I reached the finish at Little Venice Canal Basin in London, sopping wet and thoroughly fed up, I was glad that the whole thing was over. Six hours and five minutes of constant rain had not been my favourite race experience! But my fellow runners and all the volunteers involved with the race had been great company, and their

WHAT IF?

support and encouragement helped get me to the end.

So, what was my little secret that I'd kept tight-lipped about? Well, back in early 2021 – while I was nursing my poorly calf – I'd entered the ballot for a 100k race in France called the Courmayeur – Champex – Chamonix, more commonly known as the CCC. This forms part of the wider Ultra-trail Du Mont Blanc race week, cantered around the little Alpine town of Chamonix. For a week in late August, this beautiful French resort becomes a Mecca for the great, the good, and the have-a-go heroes of the trail running world as they do battle with the mountain region surrounding the Mont Blanc massif. I'd actually entered the CCC ballot in 2020, but I'd been rejected. When entry for the 2021 event came around, despite being injured at the time, I thought I'd try my luck. I suspected that I wouldn't get in once again, but what the heck, it was worth a try. Well, bugger me! Would you believe it, I got accepted! This news was both fantastic and depressing at the same time. Fantastic because I'd secured a place in one of the world's greatest mountain trail races, and depressing at the same time because in my current (non-running state), it was highly unlikely that I would have any chance of making it to the start line, let alone finishing the race. With that in mind, I told no one and forgot all about it. It wasn't until around 6 or 8 weeks before the race was due to happen that I gave it another thought. If you remember back to Summer 2021, Europe was still in the grip of the Coronavirus pandemic, and travel was not easy, and nor was staging major events of any kind for that matter. One can only assume that because of this, the organisers of the UTMB events presented that year's runners with three options. One, we could keep our race places and take part in the 2021 events under Covid-19 restrictions. Two, have our entry fee refunded. Or three, defer our 2021 entry to 2022. I couldn't believe my luck! Without a moment's hesitation, I deferred my entry to 2022. By then, fingers crossed, the pandemic would be over, I'd be injury-free, and I would have a whole 14 or so months to prepare for the CCC. That is unheard of. Usually, entrants are only given about seven months preparation time following confirmation of their race entry. With a spring in my step and uncontrollable excitement building up inside me, I confessed all to Jane. Within 24 hours, we'd secured return flights to Geneva, and hotel accommodation in Chamonix. My biggest running challenge to date was on the horizon, and endless miles of hill training were about to begin.

One of my first tasks was to spend many hours at my laptop, searching for a collection of 2022 trail races that would involve plenty of elevation gain. Following the Country to Capital, my first real uphill test would be the Endurancelife CTS South Devon 50k Ultra in early February. Starting in the small village of Beesands, the route followed uneven, technical, coastal paths before heading inland, over some tough Devon hills. This indeed was going to be a test! But, long before this race, I'd spent the winter months running over the beautiful rolling hills of the South Downs and the steep, rutted climbs of the Fairlight Glens, near my home. The Glens are particularly great when it comes to training for hilly trail races because the ascents and descents are uneven, slippery, and often involve uneven steps. I spent many hours slipping and sliding my way through those hills during the winter, slowly getting fitter and faster over the jagged terrain. I'd also spent many hours jogging up and down the steps of Hastings (trust me, there are many) trying to strengthen my leg muscles for what was to come. So, when I arrived for the start of my Devon adventure, I was feeling quietly confident.

That confidence began to fade when the route reached the first of the coastal paths, on a bright, but very blowy day. I'd run on cliff paths before, but the ones where I train have a fair bit of land between you and the sea. On this route, things were very different. With the wind whistling all around me and often gusting, I frequently found myself perilously close to a sheer drop down to the sea, and for the first time in my running life, I was feeling uncomfortable in my surroundings, and somewhat out of my depth. This was not going to plan at all. Suffice to say, I was glad when the route turned inwards, and there was much more land around me. Though the hills were very tough, I was at least in more familiar, and secure surroundings. One of the race's hardest moments came as I approached the marathon distance. Though I couldn't see the finish itself, I could hear the announcer welcoming home race finishers as I myself reached a sign that pointed to the finish in one direction and the ultra-route in the other. I still had nearly 10k to run, traversing rocks, steps, and rutted coastal path before my race was finished, and I was shattered! And yet, the finish was tantalizingly close by. It took all the strength I could muster to not turn towards the finish line. That last 10k seemed to take forever, and I was battling cramp all of the way. Reaching a sign that read "one mile to go" was manna from heaven. Finally, reaching the end, broken but happy, my joyous thoughts quickly changed. Today had been a lesson – and not a very comfortable one. If I thought I'd been training hard to this point, things were going to have to get much harder if I were to stand a chance of finishing the CCC. This race had around 6000ft of elevation gain – the CCC has 20000ft over only double the distance. Where was that quiet confidence now!

Training during the weeks following my trip to Devon involved even more hills and even more miles, as well as keeping up my regular tempo and speed sessions. By now, I was doing as many of my long runs as I could manage, off-road. In early April, I ran the Centurion South Downs Way 50-mile race for the second time. And, on a sunny but chilly spring day, surrounded by endless spectacular views, I set a new fifty-mile PB of 7:05:29. Considering the legs were tired from all of the training miles I'd been running, I was pretty pleased with that, and it was a boost to my confidence, which had taken a bit of a battering on the coastal paths of South Devon. As the saying goes, onwards and upwards – quite literally!

CHAPTER 20

THAMES PATH 100

There was one anomaly among all of the hilly races of 2022 in the shape of the Centurion Thames Path 100. This would be the flattest 100-mile race I'd tackled by far, and it was set to be a different challenge on legs that are used to undulating trails. My main concerns revolved around my pacing strategy. My previous 100s had included plenty of hills where I would walk and take on some food whilst admiring the views. But the Thames Path 100, running from Richmond to Oxford is flat – very flat. I'd heard people talking about strategies such as running for 10 minutes, then walking for 2 minutes, so that you replicate the walking breaks you might get on a hillier race. That seemed like a pretty good plan, and one I thought I could utilize. That was until – when I was volunteering at another Centurion race – I got talking to a chap who'd run the TP100 before. When I asked him how he had approached the run, his reply was, "It's a running race, isn't it? So, you run it." That got me thinking; maybe I should try and run it. If I separated the race into sections between aid stations and seeing Jane at crew points, maybe I could run it. If I kept my heart rate low, running at a very gentle pace then yes, I reckon I could do that. As long as I stayed mentally strong and stuck to a steady rate of progress, this might just work. So it was, with a plan in place, I rocked up to Richmond in Southwest London, on a bright Spring Day ready to follow the meandering path that runs alongside the river Thames. But not before Jane and I had stopped for coffee and a croissant!

I started the race exactly as planned, at a very gentle pace. Chatting to my fellow runners, remembering to drink every few miles, and generally enjoying the wildlife, views, and boats along the Thames. Basically, running without a care in the world really, so that by the time I reached the first aid station in Walton, I was feeling fine and dandy. This serene progress continued, and by the time I'd passed the quarter distance, I felt in control, and my heart rate hadn't gone above the easy zone according to my watch. I was jogging along, maintaining a nice even pace, sticking to my strategy, and feeling very much at peace with the world. Halfway arrived in the posh surroundings of Henley on Thames – all striped blazers, Pimm's and straw boaters and me and my fellow runners dodging in and out of the day trippers and locals, as we crossed from one side of the Thames to the other. Jane met me at the Henley aid station, and it was rather nice to enjoy a sandwich together by the side of the river. Our very own midrace picnic by the Thames!

The sunshine of the day had begun to turn into the dusk of the evening when I next saw Jane, 58 miles into the race in Reading. It was here that I'd decided to have a complete change of clothes, freshen-up with some baby wipes, a bit of food, and to brush my teeth. This happens at every 100-mile race I do, and Jane and I have got it down to a fine art now. The whole process is completed in about 10 minutes, and I leave feeling refreshed, revitalised, and ready for the second half of the race. After a 10-minute stop, the legs are a little stiff when I get going, but with a little gentle persuasion, they soon get moving again.

I'd already run the rest of the route during the Autumn 100, and a recce of the course that I'd done in February, so I knew that there were a few gentle hills to come over the next 10 miles or so. As darkness fell, I can tell you that my legs really enjoyed the brief change in undulation. Personally, I find running on a continually flat route quite monotonous and tough on my legs, so it was good to see some hills. This was the section of the route where I'd passed the chaps with the brazier on the Autumn 100, but alas, they were nowhere to be seen today! By the time I'd reached the pretty town of Goring, darkness had taken over, and my headtorch was on. There is an aid station here located in the beautiful town hall, and it was a very welcome sight. A quick pitstop and some words of encouragement from the always supportive Centurion volunteers and I was off into the darkness, to face one of the loneliest sections of the Thames Path.

The final 30 miles of the Thames 100 passes through lots of fields as well as towpath, and there are very few villages or towns to be found. During the whole of the final 30 miles, I only came across two of my fellow racers, and I don't think I've ever felt quite such a sense of isolation as I did on that night. It's times like this that it's reassuring to know that I, and all of the other runners are being continuously tracked throughout the whole of the race. It's also a blessed relief to periodically see Jane and the volunteers at the aid stations too. Little do they know the impact they had on my race. Seeing them provides me with a real boost and the impetus to keep going, safe in the knowledge that in under 10 miles, I'll come across one or the other of them once again. I really couldn't have done that last 30 without them. Oh, and there was one other, rather bizarre encouraging voice during the late evening hours. Running through a particularly lonely part of the Thames path, I heard a very well-spoken voice shout out, "Well done, keep going!" I looked around but couldn't see anyone. I shouted out, "Thank you, where are you?" The reply came back, "We're on the river!" There was a hedge between the Thames and me, meaning I had no idea anyone was there. I can only assume that they had spotted my headlamp coming towards them in the distance. Their encouragement was somewhat unexpected but most welcome!

The last time I saw Jane before the finish was in the town of Abingdon, where I had run a marathon a few years ago. The town is about 10 miles from the finish, and I was feeling broken and exhausted by this stage. It was at this point that I had my now customary moment of "I can't do this" It sounds daft, I know when you consider that I've already completed 90% of the race, but I can tell you that it is a very real feeling, and as I sat on a bench overlooking the Thames, I genuinely thought I couldn't take another step. Though I was feeling sick, I did manage to eat a banana, and after gentle words of encouragement from my always patient, incredible wife, I stood up and started on my way. Fortunately – to date – these feelings of doubt towards the end of a race have been but a fleeting moment. But they are genuine, and if it wasn't for Jane, I might well have stopped. Luckily, I didn't, and instead, I gave myself a pep talk, and got on with the final 10 miles.

By the time I reached the finish, my legs were trashed, and the lights of the finish shone like a beautiful beacon as I approached them. I'm sure I say the same thing after every hard race, but I've never been more pleased to reach the end. I crossed the line in 6th place in a new one hundred mile best of 16:39:41. My finishers buckle was given to me by a real Ultra-running hero of mine. His name is Rob, and he epitomizes everything that is great about ultra-distance running. When he races, he always gives it everything he's got, completely emptying the tank, and he has a determination that I can only wonder at. And, when he isn't racing, he can often be found volunteering at an aid station and supporting and encouraging his fellow Centurions. He is an inspiration to me, and it was an honour to receive my buckle from him.

All in all, the race had been a huge success. I'd stuck to my strategy, and my heart rate had only left the easy zone for a few hours during the warmth of the mid-afternoon sun. I couldn't have asked or expected much more than that.

A memory I will always treasure came a few days after the race. During a Centurion podcast the following week, the race was debriefed, and I got a mention! The presenter had said that at the first aid station, I'd been around 100th place in the race, and by the finish, I was 6th. Aid stations aside, my pace had consistently stayed at around 10 minutes per mile, and in this guy's opinion, it proved what consistency could do. I was proud as punch; I can tell you! My own 15 minutes of fame!

I followed up the TP100 with a second crack at the South Downs Way 100 in June. I think it's fair to say that this is my favourite 100-mile race. The route is stunning, with amazing views and rolling hills, and I never tire of running it. It was made even more special this time because I was joined in the last third of the race by firstly my friend Dan (remember him from the Brighton marathon), followed by my cousin Lucy who kept me company during the last 12 miles of the race. She is a fantastic runner in her own right, winning many obstacle course races. Jogging along with Lucy, ever smiling and chatting along beside me, was just what I needed to make it to the end. My wife Jane and Dan joined us for the final 300 metres around a lap of the track at Eastbourne College, and we crossed the finish line hand in hand. If ever a moment summed up the teamwork that goes into these races, this was it. I'm the one who receives the finish buckle and the congratulatory words, but it's often the unnoticed people in the background who are the real heroes of these races. The organisers, the volunteers, the family and friends who patiently and willingly give their love, support, and time to help me reach the end. Whatever I've achieved during the last seven years, I am forever indebted to these incredible people for all of the help they've given me.

As I returned to the endless miles, training alone, up and down infinite hills, my thoughts turned to what would be my toughest race to date. Mount Snowdon was calling!

CHAPTER 21

STILL HIGHER!

The mission facing me as I stood with my fellow runners at the start of the Snowdon24 challenge was simple: Reach the summit of the mountain, via the Llanberis path, as many times as you can in 24 hours. What could be easier? There were solo competitors and teams with up to 5 people in them lined up alongside me at the start. But however you were taking on the task, as part of a team or on your own, the challenge was still a big one. The Llanberis path is the easiest – but longest ascent – up Mount Snowdon, often used by tourists, those taking on the Three Peaks Challenge, and various other fundraising heroes. Race day in early July was no exception, and as the challenge began at midday, on a hot and humid summer day, the mountain was heaving.

My plan was a straightforward one; this was going to be the best chance I had of closely replicating the terrain and elevation gain that I would face in Chamonix. So, I was going to employ exactly the same tactics as I would be using during the CCC. That meant hiking up the mountain and running back down. Even on the shallowest parts of the ascent, I was resolved to doing nothing but hike.

The first two climbs up the hill were crowded and very hot, and I found myself enviously looking at those who had decided to take the steam train that goes up the mountain instead of trudging up the hill, sweating like mad. Let the train take the strain – as they used to say! If you've ever taken a stroll on the Llanberis path, you'll know that it is very exposed. This means that you are open to the elements, be they wind, rain, snow, or in my case, blazing hot sunshine. There was an event village back in the town of Llanberis from which you started and returned on each leg, and it was great to get back down there to restock on drinks and food, safe in the knowledge that another return trip was done. In the oppressive conditions, I was going through a litre of water on each nine-mile round trip. Actually, when I say water, what I really mean is ½ a litre of coke (also known as rocket fuel!) in one of my chest bottles, and ½ a litre of energy drink in the other. I find that a combination of the two, along with an energy gel on each leg, is enough to keep me moving. Back at base camp, it was either sandwiches, crisps, biscuits, or whatever took my fancy.

By the time I started my third ascent, the stifling temperatures of the day had begun to ease, and as day turned into dusk and I hiked over the rocks and shale on the way up the hill, I was treated to the most incredible sunset. A kaleidoscope of reds, oranges, and yellows filled the evening sky, and the spectacular views of the Eryri National Park were visible all around. From grey, rocky mountain tops to craggy ridges, lush green valleys, and sparkling lakes, it was an awe-inspiring sight. As I began my third descent, about halfway down, you could see the lights of Llanberis town begin to illuminate in the distance. The mountain was much quieter now, and I imagined people sat in pub gardens and restaurants, tucking into a hard-earned meal and a celebratory drink after ascending the 1000 metres to the top of the mountain. Making sure to get their obligatory photo at the top before returning to the bottom.

I summited the mountain twice overnight, and this was the first time I'd ever experienced mountain conditions during the darkness of the small hours. Though it'd been very hot during the day, overnight it was much cooler, and at the summit, there was a real chill in the air. So much so, that I found myself putting on extra clothing and spending as little time as possible at the top. The event village had changed too. During the day, it had been full of noise from the stalls, supporters, music, and event volunteers. Through the night, the lights (save for a few) were all off, the stalls were closed, and most of the support crews had disappeared. Inside the competitor's tent, there were runners asleep on benches, using coats and race vests as pillows, and some had even gone off to find their own tents so they could get a few hours' sleep before tackling the mountain once again. I'd decided that I would press on through the night without stopping, keeping my rests stops down to a minimum. After all, this was a dress rehearsal for the CCC, and I wasn't planning to stop for long out in the Alps.

As I started my sixth hike up to the peak, dawn was beginning to break. About halfway up the mountain, I found myself entering some low-lying clouds. In the quiet and the chill of early dawn, it was quite eerie. I happened to be passing a marshal at the time, and I commented to him who how wonderful this all was. He replied, "you wait until you get above the clouds." Sure enough, once I'd made my way out of the damp mist, I was treated to one of the most breathtaking sights I have ever seen. Suddenly the clouds cleared to reveal a pale blue, watery, early morning sky, and below me, the fluffy white clouds revealed the grey and green of the mountain tops peeking through. With the sun beginning to glow yellow behind them, this really was one of the most impressive sights I had ever seen. There was no one else in sight at the time, and I remember thinking to myself, I may be tired, my legs might be struggling to climb up a mountain that seems to be getting steeper with every ascent, but right now, there is nowhere else in the world I would want to be than right here! For only the second time during a race, I pulled out my phone, so I could forever capture this moment.

I would climb Mount Snowdon one last time after that, giving me a grand total of 7 ascents in 19:06:10, good enough for third overall in the solo category. But none of that really mattered. What really mattered was that I'd completed 105 kilometres and just under 7000m of ascent. More – on both counts – than I would face at the CCC. Though I was exhausted, and my legs were so sore, it appeared that the endless hours of training were paying off. I'd proved to myself that I could do this, and it was a massive confidence boost. I'd never taken part in a mountain race before and I'd been pretty apprehensive in the days leading up to the start. But I'd done ok. Better than I thought I would. I just needed to stay focused in the 7 or so weeks I had left before the CCC, and I would give myself a fighting chance of actually finishing this thing! The overweight, arrogant, undertrained Ash from the 2016 London Marathon seemed like a distant memory. I couldn't believe how far I had come.

There was a reason why I had stopped after 19 hours (aside from the fact I was physically and mentally broken and didn't have another ascent in me!). On the Sunday morning, Jane would be running the Snowdon half marathon, and I was desperate to see her finish. We were staying quite close to the race HQ, and so I was able to go back to our chalet, eat, have a shower, and get a couple of hours' rest before going to see Jane run. The conditions on race day were even tougher than they had been for the Snowdon24, and it was blisteringly hot! By the time I saw Jane, at the bottom of the Llanberis path, about 10 miles into the race, she was cooked. But she wasn't about to quit, and it was great to see her finish the race a little later. It had been a tough race, and she'd done so well. As I remember, the first thing we did was to get some ice cream!

I would have one final preparation race before heading off to Chamonix, in the shape of the Exmoor Trail Challenge. A 53km race with 2447m of ascent. The race, starting near Porlock in Somerset, fell three weeks after the Snowdon24. By the time race day came around, I was fully recovered, feeling good and looking forward to running somewhere new. The route was a stunning mixture of woodland, open farmland, coastal trails, and moorland – oh, and a stretch of energy-sapping, lactic-inducing beach near the end of the race! The section across Exmoor really didn't disappoint! As the race climbed towards Dunkery Beacon (the highest point on Exmoor) a moody mist swirled in, it was damp underfoot, and the air was distinctly chilly. I almost expected a policeman to appear out of the mist to tell me that there was an escaped convict on the moor, and I should mind where I was going!

I had a really strong race, doing my usual thing of trying to maintain a consistent pace throughout the run. Jane was crewing for me, and following on from my result in Snowdonia, I was feeling good. I made steady progress, and as I was approaching the last 5 or 6 miles along a beautiful coastal path, a passing dog walker said to me, "I think you're in third place mate." An unexpected but pleasant surprise and fairly soon, I'd caught and passed the chap in second place. Shortly after the aforementioned (and oh so tough) beach portion of the race, I could see the leader in the distance. Over the next few minutes, I began to gain ground on him quite rapidly, and with about two miles to go, I was on his tail. Suddenly I was in new territory. I'd never challenged for a race win before, and if I was reading this guy's body language correctly, he was tiring, and appearing to be struggling more than I was. With that, I made my move! I passed him, saying, "Well done – keep going," and I didn't look back. There is no comfort in looking back. I can't change what he is doing, the only influence I have right now is over me. The best thing I can do is to look forward and keep pushing as hard as possible. By the time I'd ascended the last steep climb, the route taking a sharp right turn, I allowed myself a quick glance behind me. I'd pulled out about 50 metres lead, and I only had a downhill run through some woods to come, and he was still to climb the steep hill that I'd already navigated. And so it was, a mile or so later, I crossed the finish for my first-ever race win! To say I was thrilled is an understatement! I'd never won anything in my life, save for a Clubman of the Year award when I was playing schoolboy football (and we all know what Clubman of the Year means!).

After the race, I met up with the gentleman I'd passed, and we shook hands before he told me that he was feeling shattered and broken when I passed him, and he could offer no response. I offered him my congratulations on a fine run, and Jane and I went off to find some well-earned fish & chips!

Except for a few weeks of tapering, the Exmoor Challenge brought the training and preparation races to an end, and the next time I would find myself lining up for the start of a race would be in Chamonix. It had been a hell of a ride so far, and I couldn't wait for the final flourish.

CHAPTER 22

THE CCC

Jane and I arrived in Chamonix on a warm sunny day in late August, and there wasn't a cloud to be seen in the sky. The air was fresh and clean, and Chamonix, with its beautiful Alpine buildings, sparkling river carrying crystal clear water down from the mountains, and breathtaking surroundings were a picture of perfection. We'd arrived 2 days before the race, and there were runners milling about the town, many making their way to the event village where they could spend a small fortune buying last-minute running kit from shoes to head torches and running vests, as well as UTMB-branded souvenirs aplenty! Some of the races that make up the UTMB race week had already started, and some had already finished by the time we arrived. The world's best trail runners were in town, giving interviews, signing autographs, and posing for pictures. We'd been told what to expect when we arrived in this little French town, but we weren't quite prepared for this. Endless UTMB flags, signs, and banners, giant TV screens that would broadcast the races as they happened, and the famous UTMB finishing arch positioned in front of the pretty little Saint Michel church, which would be waiting to welcome weary runners home after a trip through the mountains. I wondered for a moment whether or not I'd be one of them? The atmosphere was intoxicating, and if we weren't already excited enough, we certainly were now. The plan was to spend the next two days exploring Chamonix and the nearby mountain range before my race, and no sooner had we checked into our hotel, we were off on our adventures. We took a cable car up to the Le Brevent mountain from where we got our first glimpse of the Mont Blanc massif opposite us, rising out of the valley floor. The snow-covered peak looked majestic against the pale blue afternoon sky, rising proudly and boldly above the rest of the mountain range; it was an incredible sight to behold. I'd experienced mountains back home in the UK, but nothing like this. Both Jane and I stood, gazing in amazement at the beauty and wonder of it all. Over the next two days, in between picking up my race number and browsing through the event village and outdoor shops, we would find ourselves gazing up at the mountains again, and again. They truly were mesmerizing, and Jane and I were in awe of our surroundings.

The day before the CCC, I had to go through the mandatory race kit inspection required by the race organisers, which I can promise you is a very nerve-wracking experience. Woe betides any runner who has forgotten one of the required pieces of kit. I'm pleased to say that I passed with flying colours, and once this is done, you can pick up your race number and tracker. With my number now firmly in my hand, this was all starting to feel very real, and the nerves were beginning to build. Time to carb-load on some of the delicious food that was on offer in the town, and then try and get some much-needed sleep. Less than 24 hours to go before the biggest running challenge of my life!

Race day morning arrived with the sound of my early morning alarm clock. It need not have bothered; I was wide awake anyway. The sun that we'd enjoyed on our first two days in France had now given way to grey skies and heavy clouds. I had to catch an early morning coach for the trip from Chamonix, across the border into Italy, via the Mont Blanc tunnel, to the small town of Courmayeur, where the race would start. My fellow runners were gathered around the town nervously fidgeting and checking, then rechecking their race kit, and I was no different. The tension was broken for me in the queue for the toilets of all places. I turned around and recognised the man standing behind me. It was none other than author Adharanand Finn. I'd read all three of his running books, including his latest – The Rise of the Ultrarunners. Over the many miles of training I'd done, that book had kept me company, inspired me – and filled me with dread – in equal measures! Adharanand's book culminates in him running the main event of UTMB week, the famous 100-mile race along the whole of the Ultra trail du Mont Blanc. But today he was joining us on the 100k CCC. It was great to chat with him, and for a brief while, it took my mind off thoughts of the challenge to come. Selfie taken and shared with Jane; my mind was soon back to thoughts of the race and the steep mountain climbs that awaited me.

It seemed to take an interminably long time for the start to arrive, but finally it came, and it was time to make my way into the starting pens. The excitement was building, the crowds were gathering, and there was deafening music being played through loudspeakers while we waited for the starting gun to go. The race announcer was talking enthusiastically in French with what I guess were words of encouragement. It turns out my French really isn't that good after all, because I had no idea what she was saying! In any event, those that could understand were cheering and clapping enthusiastically as she spoke. She did inform us in English that rain was forecast, and that we may get the odd thunderstorm during the race! As if this wasn't going to be hard enough already, I thought! Suddenly, a countdown began, and before I knew it, we were on our way, running through the streets of Courmayeur. After months of preparation, running endless miles, and climbing thousands of feet, my mountain adventure was finally underway.

The houses and streets of Courmayeur soon gave way to

mountain trails. The first climb was long and tough, and I found myself a link in a chain of slowly moving runners. The trail was single track only, and our convoy often came to a grinding halt as we waited for those in front to move up the mountain. I'd expected the hills to be steep, but this was quite an introduction. For those who have walked up the Llanberis path to the summit of Mount Snowdon, you'll know there is a steep section of climb following the second railway bridge. It's hard work, and you can really feel it pulling on your calf muscles. It's a fairly brief section of the hike, but you know you've done it. The first climb of the CCC was like that section nearly the whole way up. This was a real baptism of fire, and I found myself reaching and pulling on my walking poles as I trudged up the endless, never-ending path. The climb went on and on, and after what felt like an age, I finally reached Tete de la Tronche, and the first summit, around 10k into the race. Unbelievably, just as I arrived at the top, the threatened storm arrived with a huge clap of thunder! Before the race, I was terrified of this happening on these exposed mountains, thinking I might be fried by an errant lightning bolt! But when the lightning did fill the sky, all I could do was laugh to myself. I mean, the timing was priceless! Between Tete de la Tronche and the first aid station, you run along the most incredible ridge. Sitting high up in the mountain range, with steep slopes on either side, it is the most breathtaking of places. Running along the narrow path, passing avalanche fences along the way, the views are spectacular. Though the cloudy skies were blocking a lot of the views, the dark, commanding grey silhouettes of the mountains were still visible. Of all the places I've been lucky enough to run, this ridge really was amongst the most impressive. I felt on top of the world, running with the birds alongside me, and I swear if I'd reached out, I could've touched them. The ridge was over all too quickly, and before long, I was on the alarmingly steep descent into the first rest stop at Refuge Bertone.

The aid station was rammed with runners, all reaching for food and trying to get water bottles refilled. The patiently smiling and ever-

WHAT IF?

willing volunteers, communicating in broken English to runners of various nationalities, tried desperately to keep everyone fed and watered as swiftly as possible. They really do a first-class job, in very difficult circumstances, and I for one know that I am forever indebted to them. Once I'd had my fill, I set off once again, still gobsmacked by the magnificence of my surroundings. A few kilometres later, the rain began to fall. Steadily at first, but quickly getting harder. The conditions underfoot changed rapidly from dry compacted earth to slippery wet mud, making for treacherous progress along the narrow trails. Onwards we went through valleys and lush green pastures, past rivers, across rickety wooden bridges, and over mountains before reaching the second rest stop at Arnouvaz, some 26k into the race. And, if I'd thought the first rest stop was chaos, this was on another level! It was like being in a London underground station during rush hour. Only with more food and wet floors! Still, the delicious continental cuisine spread out before my eyes more than made up for the anarchy. The salami was particularly delicious! I wasn't spending much time in the aid stations though, preferring to keep moving; I seemed to be passing no end of other runners, who just couldn't seem to tear themselves away from the culinary delights on offer. Not long after leaving Arnouvaz, the climb up to the Grand Col Ferret began, where at the top, we would reach the highest point of the race. As with the first ascent, the climb to the top of this mountain seemed to go on forever – even longer than the first if that were possible. Reaching up into the mist, ever higher. But much to my delight, the summit finally appeared out of the clouds, and as I reached the volunteers stationed at the top, by way of relief, I just had to say, "Buongiorno!" "No, no," came the reply, "you're in Switzerland now, it's bonjour!" It's the first time I've ever crossed into another country with no checkpoint or border controls! To be honest, I'm not even sure where on earth the border had been.

Running from La Fouly to Champex-Lac, I'd been lulled into a false sense of security. The terrain had been mainly flat or downhill, over firm trails and roads, making for fast progress. But things were about to change. Shortly after leaving the aid station, the uphill climbs returned. And now, instead of smooth trails and tarmac, I was confronted with rocks, boulders, and stream crossings. This was steep – very steep, very technical and like nothing I'd seen before. More than once I slipped and staggered as the loose surface beneath my feet kept moving. Luckily, I caught up with some runners ahead of me, and I was able to follow their footsteps as we made our way up the hill. Finally, we reached the top of the mountain, which opened up onto high green pastures, where herds of cattle were chewing the fresh grass while their bells, hanging from beautifully decorated leather collars, clanged and rung. Passing by the inquisitive cows, we reached the next aid station, which was nothing more than a barn with plastic barrels of water racked up inside it, in the middle of nowhere. Leaving the barn, I followed the course markings down through yet another rocky, technical, steep descent. This made my aching quads even angrier, as the sharp downward slopes began to take their toll. So, it was a relief when I reached the little town of Trient, with its pretty pink church in the centre of the village, about 70k into the race. Jane and I had planned to meet here too, but as I entered the rest stop, she was nowhere to be seen. I filled my water bottles and ate some food, all the time glancing about, hoping to see her. I was just about to message Jane to say that I was fine and that I was leaving, and I'd catch up with her at the next aid station, when I heard her call out. She'd been delayed and had only just arrived. I can tell you it was a huge relief to see her. I would've been ok, of course, but I always look forward to seeing Jane, and somehow it puts a spring in my step, and after seeing her, I feel ready to tackle the next part of the race.

Shortly after leaving Trient, darkness fell as day turned into night, and the stars began to shine and twinkle overhead. I'd put on a warmer top as I left Trient along with my headtorch, and as I climbed through a beautiful pine forest, with that lovely pine tree smell hanging in the air, the headtorch went on, lighting up the trail beneath me. The path twisted and turned its way up through the trees, and I was relieved to find that this hill wasn't as steep as the previous one. Or at least it didn't feel as steep to me. By the time I'd reached the next checkpoint in Vallorcine – 82k into the race – I'd reached a tipping point. It was now easier hiking up the hills than running down them. With every step, my quads were getting more painful on the descents, sending sharp pains through my legs. It was beginning to have an effect on me, and I'd begun to notice my pace slowing down. The steep drop into Vallorcine seemed to go on forever, and as I spotted the aid station in the distance, I couldn't wait for a break and some food.

This would be the final time I would see Jane before the end of the race. I was beginning to tire now, and, as ever, it was a real boost to see her. The rest stops were much quieter now than they had been in the early stages of the race. Opposite me, a few other runners sat in the marquee, many looking off into the distance, no doubt contemplating the final 20k that was still to come. As I pulled myself up from the bench, leaving the relative comfort of the giant tent behind me, I too was thinking exactly the same. How the hell was I going to reach the end?

The path out of Vallorcine rose steadily uphill, and the gentle gradient and smooth surface made it easily runnable. I wasn't moving particularly quickly, but it was at least quicker than walking. I thought to myself, if the ascent stays like this, it shouldn't be too bad. I'd been running under the cover of some trees, which abruptly opened out to reveal clear skies above me. I looked up and thought, those stars are shining brightly tonight; how beautiful they looked against the dark sky. And then, like a punch to the gut, it hit me. They were not stars at all. Instead, disappearing up into the night sky – climbing sharply – were headtorches. These were other runners ahead of me, ascending yet another steep mountain. For a moment, my heart sank. "I'm never going to be able to do this," I said to myself. My legs were broken, and the relentless up and down had taken its toll, and I was aching and tired. "Is this it?" I thought to myself. "Is this where this journey comes to an end?" At the foot of a hill, by the side of a road, 15k from the end. As I sunk onto my poles, for a brief moment, I really thought my race was run; I had nothing else to give. That was until another runner came alongside and muttered something like "keep going, you have to keep going." Those simple words were a real boost and exactly what I needed to hear; what else was there to do but keep going. And so, straightening myself up, I crossed the road and began the last steep climb of the race.

This was tough – very tough. A relentlessly steep incline, winding its way up the mountain, through continuous switchbacks, over rocks and boulders. I passed more than one runner, sitting by the side of the trail, taking a moment to gather themselves before pushing on up the hill. I offered words of encouragement as I passed, but I was determined to keep moving, albeit at a snail's pace. And, after what seemed like an eternity, I finally began cresting the hill onto the summit of the mountain. It was a joyous moment filled with a massive sense of relief – I'd made it. But that relief was short-lived. Though the mountain flattened out, the trail that stretched out in front of me was made up of large boulders and rocks. Just lifting my legs up onto them was hard enough, but stepping down was agony. My quads were screaming in pain with every downward step, and I just wanted this to end. Finally, I reached the last aid station at La Flegere. I was now 93k in – only 7k to go. But, looking down to the bright lights of Chamonix, all I could think was, "That is a long way down, how the hell am I going to make it all the way down there on these legs?" Somewhere during the night, I'd crossed the border from Switzerland into France, and now, I could see the pretty French town glowing in the distance. That meant that with one final push, this would soon be over.

The final 7k wound its way down through a wood full of loose stone and tree roots. I lost count of how many times I cursed as I tripped on another root or rock! Eventually, the trees gave way to a gravel road, leading down into the town. At last, the mountains were done. As I made my way through the streets of Chamonix, happy at last to be back on tarmac, I was greeted like a hero by the locals who were still filling the streets and the bars, some rather worse for wear in the early hours of the morning! Buoyed by their support, my pace quickened, and all the pain I'd been feeling just a few minutes earlier seemed to disappear. As I ran the final 1k to the finish, now seemingly full of energy, I couldn't wait to reach the finishing arch in front of the pretty church. Finally, after 16 and a half hours, of mountains and valleys, the UTMB finish arch came into view – I'd done it! It had nearly broken me, but somehow, I'd made it to the end.

Amongst the crowd, I saw Jane as I ran into the finish funnel, and it was so good to see her. We'd shared this journey together. She'd been with me through the hard times and the good, always supportive and always encouraging, and I couldn't have done it without her. We returned to our hotel room, tired and weary but happy. And, as I looked out of the window, I could see in the darkness, the shining lights beaming from the headtorches of the runners who were still out there, making their way down the final hill into Chamonix. There was something comforting and heart-warming in knowing that they were nearly home, safe and sound, ready to bask in the glory of what they had just achieved.

Jane and I stayed on in Chamonix for a couple of days to soak up more of the UTMB atmosphere and to watch the end of the 100-mile race. Many of those reaching the finish were joined by their families for the last few metres through the town, and watching this unfold was really quite emotional. But my lasting memory from our French adventure came at the end of the 90-mile, TDS race by way of a Welsh runner approaching the finish, carrying a Welsh flag, surrounded by friends. The crowds waiting at the finish were cheering and clapping as if she had won the race, and the actual TDS winner was waiting for her at the finish too. But she was never classified as a finisher, and you won't find her name on the official results. That is because she was outside of the race cut off times, but nevertheless, she was determined to make it to the end. That she was welcomed home as a hero goes to show how much her courage and resolve had been recognised by those watching on. If there was ever a moment that epitomised everything that is wonderful about this sport, surely this was it.

2022 came to an end in a rather unexpected way. After returning home from France, I had recovered from my exploits at the CCC quicker than expected, and I was soon doing my weekly effort and speed sessions, alongside my longer runs, once again. As well as this, I had also purchased my first pair of "go faster" carbon-plated shoes. I had resisted the temptation to buy a pair so far because these things are ludicrously expensive. But Adidas had just released their third incarnation of the Adios Pro shoe, meaning that I was able to get hold of a second-generation pair at a bargain price. I have no idea what makes these trainers so fast, and I guess I don't need to know either. The fact is that research seems to show that they can make us run faster and/or increase endurance. The first time I wore them, they felt strange, and at an easy pace, it was like trying to run in a pair of Cuban-heeled boots! But once I got up to race pace, these things came alive. Just looking down at these speedy-looking shoes made me feel faster. I had already secured a place in the London Marathon (the last one to be held in October before the race would return to its normal April date), and so I thought, let's give this thing a go. There was nothing riding on the race, and I had nothing to lose – so why not. The conditions on race day were perfect, and I felt really good. So, wearing my go-faster shoes, it was time to see what I was made of. I'm delighted to say I had the race of my life! I felt strong throughout the whole run, only really beginning to feel the pace with about three miles to go. But by then, I knew something special was happening, and I wasn't about to slow down. I crossed the line in a quite unbelievable 2:48:07, giving me a massive PB. I have no idea how I did that. Since the Abingdon Marathon in 2016, I had taken nearly 22 minutes off my marathon PB! I must've tried really hard because as I was limping away from the finish – utterly exhausted – a medic asked if I was okay. At first, I replied "yes," but then I changed my reply to "Actually, I'm ecstatic! I've just scored a massive PB!"

I followed up the success of the London Marathon by racing the Brighton 10k in November. Again, I had recovered well, and just as I had the last time I ran this race, I had tweaked my training to include shorter, faster, tempo and speed runs. Race day was greeted by bright sunny weather, but there was a bit of a breeze in the air. But regardless of the conditions, I was determined to give this my best shot. Warming up before the race, I was nervous but feeling unusually confident for me. Once again, wearing the super shoes, I had another great run. The sort of run that only happens once in a while when you feel like you're floating instead of running. The last 2 kilometres were brutal, and I had to fight fatigue and negative thoughts to hang on. But hang on I did, finishing in 35:49, taking 1 minute 13 seconds off my previous best. I hate short races, so to say I was happy would be an understatement. At 50 years old, I had set a new 10k PB!

Now I know what you're thinking, the big question is, why was I faster? After years of hard training, was I fitter, or was it down to the shoes? If I may be so bold, I'd like to think it was a little of both! But whatever the reason, I'm just pleased to have improved on my personal bests! 2022 really had been a special year, and this brought it to a fitting, if somewhat surprising end.

CHAPTER 23

ONE LAST DANCE

If 2022 had finished on a high, 2023 started in more worrying circumstances. Having recently turned 50, I received a random text message from the NHS suggesting that I might want to have a blood pressure test, just to check that everything was functioning as normal, and that I was fit and healthy. Thinking nothing of it, I arranged for a test and duly went along to my local town hall at the given date and time. The test was carried out, and to my surprise, I was told the reading was high, and I might want to make an appointment with my doctor so that they could take a closer look. This was worrying, to say the least, and to say this was a surprise is an understatement. I was as fit as I'd ever been in my life, and this was the last thing I expected. I made an appointment to see my GP before I got home. I then spent a worrying two weeks, doing completely the wrong thing by searching on Google in an attempt to find out what was wrong with me. By the time I made it to the doctor's surgery, I was convinced that I was about to die! The nurse who carried out the test was very kind, and she happened to ask how many times my blood pressure had been recorded during my previous test. Much to her chagrin, I told her that it was once. "Once," she said, "was never an accurate enough test, and she would do it three times over a few minutes, and then look at the average readings." Needless to say, it turns out that my blood pressure is fine. These three separate checks showed that nothing was wrong. However, there was a twist in the plot! While carrying out the test, she'd noticed that my resting heart rate was unusually low, and she asked if I'd noticed that too? My Garmin watch tells me that my resting heart rate averages about 48 bpm, which apparently is low. This meant that the nurse wanted to make a further appointment for me so that I could be attached to something known as an ECG machine. This would show if my heart was functioning normally. This was all beginning to get very alarming, and it wasn't a great start to my fifties! A few days later, I was back at the surgery, with all sorts of pads on my chest attached to a box that was bleeping and flashing in the corner. It was all over very quickly, and I nervously awaited the results. That, as it turned out, was somewhat naïve. The nurse only carried the procedure, and a doctor would need to check over the results of the test. Anyway, after a few days of anxious waiting and worrying, I received a phone call. My doctor had looked at the results and he was happy that everything was normal, putting my low resting heart rate down to the fact that I was fit for my age. The relief I felt was overwhelming. I'd had all sorts of thoughts racing through my mind. Anything from, I could have a heart attack at any moment, to I'm at death's door or worse still - what if I couldn't run anymore!? All's well that ends well, as they say, but it had been a wake-up call, and a reminder to keep a check on my health. Before these blood pressure tests, I hadn't seen my doctor for about 8 years. I won't be waiting that long again!

Health worries over, thoughts turned to running once again. There was no way that '23 could live up to '22, and as the year began, I wasn't sure what my race plans might be, though they quickly began to take shape. I knew I had a place in the London Marathon, but there wasn't a lot else on the horizon during the early part of the year. That was until I received an email saying that I had a place in the Brighton Marathon. To be honest, I'd completely forgotten about it. I must have entered it at some time, but it'd slipped my mind. These issues with turning 50 were growing by the day! I'm starting to forget things now! The future of the Brighton Marathon had been in question at the start of 2023. It transpired that there had been a dispute involving unpaid prize money for previous race winners, and it quickly became apparent that the owners of the race were in financial difficulties. It would've been a real shame to see this race disappear because since its inception, it had become the leading marathon on the South Coast. Luckily, the organisers of the London Marathon stepped in and agreed to take over the running of the event. And so it was that I unexpectedly lined up for the start of the Brighton Marathon in April, once again.

It was good to be back at the place where I broke 3 hours for the first time after a 5-year absence. It is my local marathon, and I have quite a soft spot for it. I just wish that it could've been a bit warmer. As I stood with everyone else, waiting for the start, I was freezing! Covered in goose pimples, and frantically jumping up and down in an effort to stay warm, I couldn't wait for the start to arrive. I'd never felt this cold in my life. Once out on the course, as usual the Brighton Marathon didn't disappoint. Supporters and musicians were lining the streets with their drums and their cheers enthusiastically making a deafening noise. And after the initially chilly temperatures, it began to warm up, and the sun made an appearance too. I thoroughly enjoyed the race and eventually crossed the finish line in a time of 2:48:54. I must admit that I was pleasantly surprised with that because I wasn't sure how well my training had gone. Must've been something to do with those fast shoes again! It wasn't until I got home that I'd realised I'd finished 41st overall and first out of 901 entrants in the M50 category. If you had told me before the race that I would've done that, I doubt I have believed you. First in my age group in a major city marathon was just mad!

One of the things that stood out from my race was my negative split. As I previously mentioned, I wasn't sure how my training block had gone. That meant I approached the race very cautiously. My confidence must've grown in the second half of the race because I ended up being nearly 6 minutes faster over the second 13.1 miles! That is definitely not the right way to run a negative split. I'd been way too cautious in the first half of the race. The thing is, it's in my nature to be a very cautious person in all walks of my life. Who knows why? Is it our upbringing or maybe our past that determines these things? Perhaps what it does go to show is that my running is nothing more than an extension of my already cautious personality.

Three weeks after Brighton, I completed what I think is my 13th lap around the streets of London. As was the case on the previous twelve occasions, I found the whole thing exhilarating, inspirational, moving, and uplifting. Actually, I suspect that if I ran the London Marathon 13 times more, I would still be overwhelmed by this incredible event. It most certainly is by far and away my favourite city marathon.

I returned to the trails in June with my second attempt at the 50k Weald Challenge. I can only reiterate once again that this really is a special little run. The route is stunning, the organization is spot on, and I highly recommend giving it a go. If only for the brilliant coffee mug! I have two now and because I finished in third place this time, they gave me a porcelain plate too. If I keep this up for a few more years, I'll end up with a complete dinner service!

My next race of 2023 was the Centurion Wendover Woods 50 Miles in early July. You might recall me mentioning earlier that I'd run the 50k (31-mile) version of this race back in 2019. I'd found that challenging enough, so with the extra 20 miles, this was going to be brutal! This race normally takes place in November, but as part of a trail running weekend, it'd been moved to July for 2023. It was one of only two of the traditional Centurion races that I haven't run before. The other being the Chiltern Wonderland 50 that I would be racing in a few months' time in September, and I was using this race as a bit of a warm-up. The courses are completely different, but that didn't matter, the race mileage was what I was really after. Come to think of it, I should say that I've never run the North Downs Way 50 as a standalone race either. But the first half of the NDW100 is the same as the fifty, so in a way, I've sort of done it, right!?

The Wendover Woods 50 consists of 5 x 10-mile laps around the undulating Wendover Woods in Buckinghamshire, and it is one heck of a challenge. With a whopping elevation gain of 10,000ft, it's not for the fainthearted! Whoever designed this route must be a sadistic son of a whatsit! The worst of the hills, though short in length, are amongst the steepest gradients I've ever encountered during a run. That makes it a physically hard task, but the real test is a mental one. On a linear course, once you've conquered a demanding section of the route, you have the satisfaction of knowing it's over, but on a lapped course such as this, you know that you're going to have to do it again and again. And, to add a twist of dark humour to proceedings, the organisers like to give tough sections of the course names like the boulevard of broken dreams. Like I said, a sadistic bunch of whatsits!

The job at hand wasn't made any easier by the hot and humid weather on race day, and by the end of the second lap, I was really beginning to question my life choices! But the woods are beautiful, and the Centurion gang are just great, so it wasn't all bad. And the rain that fell during the middle part of the race was a most welcome relief. If I'm honest, I didn't have my greatest-ever run here. I got my nutritional strategy all wrong, and I wasn't drinking enough either. That meant my energy levels were depleted, making the final two laps a real slog. You'd think that by this stage I'd have these things nailed down. But it just goes to show, if you don't concentrate, a race can change very quickly. Not my finest hour. In the end, I finished in 9:22:13, good enough for 7th place. Regardless of my race performance, it had been a really great experience, and I'm so glad that I did it. What I couldn't quite get my head around was the fact that while I was wheezing and puffing my way around the 50-mile race, there were others out on the course who were in the latter stages of a 100-mile race! That's a full ten laps of this hellish course. I have absolutely no idea how any of them did it, and I am in awe of them. The truly amazing thing was that as I passed these mad runners, a lot of them were still smiling too!

In mid-September, we arrived at my goal race of the year – the Centurion Chiltern Wonderland 50. A few months previously, I'd been sitting at home, messing about on my computer, when I came across the Centurion running Hall of Fame. I found my way to the Chiltern Wonderland statistics page and discovered that the fastest ever V50 time stood at 7:55:08. "I reckon I could beat that" was the thought that sprang to mind. And that became all-consuming, all-encompassing, and almost obsessional. Every time I was out on a long training run or when I didn't want to turn out to run a hard session, I would say to myself "7:55, Ash, stay focused on 7:55" Constantly reminding myself of the ultimate goal kept my mind focused on the job in hand. I'd get over to the South Downs as often as I could because that was where I could replicate the race conditions I would face at the Chilterns most closely. By the time the race day came around, training had gone well, and though I'd had a blip at the Wendover Woods 50, I felt in pretty good shape.

"There is no one here today, Ash. You might have a chance!" That is what Centurion Running race director James Elson said to me when I arrived in Goring on Thames, on a lovely sunny day, for the start of the Chiltern 50. I smiled and laughed, of course, but I wasn't thinking about race wins. 7:55 was all I was concerned about. The route itself is spectacular. Starting beside the Thames river in Goring, the race takes in the beautiful rolling hills and valleys of the Chilterns, passing through quaint English villages such as Turville, where the

Vicar of Dibley was filmed as well as passing by the windmill seen in the film, Chitty Chitty Bang Bang. The views across the English countryside are magnificent, and for scenery, this race rivals the beauty of the South Downs Way 50. Though I must confess that for me, it doesn't quite trump it! But I might be a tad biased!

I gathered with my fellow runners down by the Thames as we waited for the race to begin. After a few anxious minutes, we were off, and I settled into a steady pace. Unusually for me, I'd started near the front of the field because I knew the start of the race would be narrow and cramped. If I was going to succeed in my ambitions today, I knew that I would need to maintain a steady but quick pace for the whole run. I had to be brave.

After a few miles, we came to the end of a path that split both left and right. The route on my watch was telling me to turn right, but the course markers were pointing left. Slightly confused, I wasn't sure what to do, but luckily, I happened to be running next to a chap who had run all the previous Chiltern Wonderland 50s, and he said it was left, definitely left. Bowing to his superior knowledge, I went left. After about a ¼ of a mile or so, I looked around to see that nobody else had gone with us. This felt very wrong, and I quickly took the decision to turn around and go back in the direction from which I had come. I soon returned to the point where I'd gone wrong, and everybody else was taking the right turn! Though this was a slight problem, it was not the time to panic, and I said to myself, "Don't start running too hard, Ash. Just Keep it steady." As the race approached the first aid station at 10 miles, I had caught up with the runners that I'd started with and settled in for the long haul – "7:55, Ash, just keep thinking 7:55."

Over the next few miles, I chatted with the people I was running alongside, admiring the views and revelling in the joy of life, until I gradually pulled ahead. As we approached the second aid station at around 18 miles, I overheard one of the volunteers exclaim, "Here comes the first runner!" The first runner? I was slightly taken aback because I hadn't realised I was leading. After my wrong turn, I had assumed the leaders were ahead, and as usual, I wouldn't catch up with them. Yet, here I was, unexpectedly in the lead. Once I wrapped my head around it, I grabbed some food, refilled my bottles, and continued along the course.

What followed over the next 32 miles can only be described as mental torture. I had rarely led a race before, let alone for over thirty miles. As is inevitable in ultra-distance races, there were many highs and lows to navigate. During rough patches, I found myself wondering about the runners behind me. Were they struggling, or were they effortlessly bounding along the trails like gazelles? Was the pack closing in, and if so, how rapidly? "I bet they aren't struggling; I just know I'll see one of them soon." This mental torment was almost unbearable. However, the miles and aid stations continued to pass, and I saw no one catching up from behind. The views and the beautiful countryside surrounding me seemed to fade as the race became solely about the competition.

Finally, I arrived at the last aid station with only 9 miles to go, and as I was filling up my bottles, one of the volunteers happened to say,

"Do you want to know how far ahead you are?" I replied, "Yes," and he said, "About 200 metres. In fact, you should be able to see the chap behind you anytime soon." This was a body blow. At the previous aid station, I'd been told I had a lead of about 4 minutes, and now this guy was only seconds away. There was no way I could hold him off. I'm starting to feel the pace now, and he's coming like a steam train. Dejected and demoralised, I set off on my way once again, anticipating the inevitable.

There is a fairly long stretch of straight road immediately after the aid station, followed by a left turn. As I reached the end of the road and took the turn, I glanced over my shoulder. I couldn't see anyone. Maybe he was resting for a while. Onwards I went, and I soon came across a rolling field, followed by another bend. This time, when I took the turn and glanced back, I could see my hunter off in the distance. I had a bigger lead than I thought. I have no idea whether or not he saw me, but I decided from that moment on, I wasn't going to give him the chance of seeing me again. My job now was to keep going and not look back.

As I approached a small wood, just a couple of miles before Goring, I still hadn't seen anyone behind me. Though it'd clearly been on my mind because I'd been pushing (probably too hard), and I was exhausted. During the last couple of miles, I have never felt such a weird disconnection between my legs and my brain. My mind was telling my legs to keep running, but they were in a world of their own. Just staying upright became a challenge! As the trees and fields gave way to houses, and I realised I was back in Goring, I finally began to believe that I might actually win this thing. Running towards Goring village hall, a place that had become very familiar over the last few years, I knew the end was in sight. A few people had gathered and were cheering and clapping as I passed the hall entrance and turned into the finish in a time of 7:29:28. Not only had I beaten the V50 course record, but I was also a Centurion race winner!

Now, I would like to point out that my finishing time was the slowest ever winning time at the Chiltern Wonderland 50 – by quite some distance I believe, but to me, that didn't matter. I was now the proud owner of one of the amazing Centurion Running trophies. I'd often glanced across at them, never thinking that I'd own one. It's only an inanimate object, I know, but it's what it represents to me that counts. Every tough training run, every moment of disappointment. The countless times I 'd got it wrong and had to go back to the drawing board. The literally thousands of miles I'd run, every injury setback that I'd suffered. This moment made it all worth it, and I will treasure it forever.

In the end, the chap who finished second came in about 4 minutes behind me. As he wandered into the village hall, I looked up to see him. He looked shattered and dejected, and I couldn't help but feel a pang of guilt. Like me, he'd given this race his all – who knows, maybe he'd tried even harder. But he was second and there would be no trophy for him to put on the mantlepiece. I walked over and congratulated him on an amazing run, and said that one day, he would be holding one of these trophies. He was generous, kind and magnanimous and we had a great chat about the race. I wasn't comfortable with how I was feeling, and I wondered whether or not I was really cut out for this sort of ruthless racing. It just didn't feel like me or what I run for.

If my memory serves me well, I think the chap who came second was called, Tom and by pushing me hard to the very end, he motivated me to be push hard too. I owe him a lot. I'm no better a runner than Tom. In fact, I'm no better than anyone. It's just that fate gave me the speed to be fast enough to win races – that is lucky on my part. Whichever race we find ourselves running, from first to last, there are stories of people who pushed their limits just to make it to the end. Going further, longer, or faster than they have ever been before, achieving things that they once thought impossible. Crossing boundaries into new territory and reaching new goals. But for the vast majority of them, there will be no winner's trophy, no name in the post-race report. But you know, winners don't always finish first. But I know you are there, I know you train just as hard as I do, if not harder. You inspire me every day, and just like Tom, I owe you a lot.

You would be forgiven for thinking that the words James spoke to me that morning before the race had begun were a little harsh, but that would be wrong. James is a straight talking man, and he says things exactly as he sees them. These were words of encouragement. Words that said, "Seize the day, Ash." And they vindicated everything I have ever said. I'm not a top athlete, and I never will be.

I'm a very ordinary runner who wondered what would be achievable if I really tried. If I worked hard to be the best I could be, where might this journey end? I guess this result goes to show what is possible with a bit of dedication, hard work, patience and a whole lot of self-belief. You just never know what can happen if you just try.

Just two weeks after the Chilterns race, I embarked on the most unusual of race challenges I'd ever encountered. I had a place in the Sri Chimnoy Self Transcendence 24 Hour Track race. The race would take place on a 400m athletics track in Battersea, London. The premise was simple you had to run around and around a 400m track as many times as you could in 24 hours. I was quite proud of the fact that I'd actually been given a place in this prestigious race. It's been an annual event for many years now and to gain entry, you have to fill out a form, listing all of your previous ultra racing experience. The race is always oversubscribed, so the organisers pick around 50 or so runners from the entrants they've received. To be selected was a big moment for me. But once I'd got over the initial excitement, it begun to dawn on me just how tough this challenge would be.

I hadn't run on a track for years. Never liked it when I had. So I knew that if I was going to have any chance of making a success of this race, I was going to have to spend a lot of time going round in circles. You see, running on a track is different. For a start it's spongier and there no elevation changes, just the same relentless flat. I'd been told that the race changed direction every four hours, which was apparently quite an exciting moment, but that would be the only change to the unrelenting monotony. Bearing this in mind, I'd started an hourly track training run, once a week and I'd also hired a local track where I could run for a few hours at time. I'd also taken part in one, six hour track race where I covered 30 miles. The one take away from all of this – my word it was boring! I mean mind-numbingly dull. How the hell was I going to keep this up for 24 bloody hours? I guess I was learning why they call it the race of transcendence!

Race day arrived in late September, and Jane and I made our way up to Battersea. My amazing wife would once again be crewing for me, and when we arrived, we were duly shown to our spot beside the track where we could park our car. The car would be our aid station for the 24 hours. Our sanctuary from the madness so to speak! Luckily, I knew two other people who would be taking part, so I had someone to talk to as we waited for the start. The race briefing done and dusted; the race began at midday on a warm and balmy Saturday, and 53 of us started on our long day.

It's difficult to know what to say about the race really. The track is located in the shadow of Battersea Power station, making for a pretty impressive back drop. But after a while, it just becomes Battersea Power station, exactly the same as the lap before. My run went quite well. I had my ups and downs as usual, but how exciting can going round and round a track be? What I can tell you is that this was the toughest physical challenge I've undertaken. Actually one of the highlights of the race was a young fox who entertained us by trying to run off with my shoes, throwing around the sand in the long jump pit, raiding people's food and at one point, trying to remove a hat from a runner who was taking a nap on a bench! But this is to sell the experience short, and I'll endeavour to explain why.

Like I said, when I arrived at the track, I knew two people. The rest were strangers, and it was a bit like the first day of school or a new job. Everyone looking around and nodding to each other. I was introduced to my lap counter who would keep an eye on my progress during the race and also the volunteers who would look after us. Once we got going, I passed my lap counter for the first time, and she said, "Well done, Ash." Then she did the same on the second lap, and then the third. In fact throughout the entire race – even when the lap counting team changed over – every time I passed them words, to that effect were passed between us. Not once, did my counters fail to encourage me and congratulate me when I reached distance milestones. The aid station volunteers were just the same. Every time I passed, they offered words of encouragement, ever smiling as they handed us food and drinks. And my fellow runners. Well, I knew only two people when I arrived, but by the end, I'd chatted to all of them, and knew many by their first names. We shared in each other's achievements, offered a kind word during the low moments. Empathised, and shared one another's pain. Even the crews who were there looking after runners became supporters of everyone. The very best of humanity was on display at a track in Battersea, and it was incredible. And thanks to each and every one of these people, I never once got bored!

Normally when we race on road or trail, we only get to see a few people. Those immediately around us, or a few that we may pass or vice versa. But this was different. By the very nature of the fact that it's only a 400m track, over a 24 hour race, you get to see the same people again and again. This means you begin to fully understand that whatever pace they are going at, whatever their ambitions are, they are giving their very best. It's humbling, inspiring and I loved it.

You may have noticed that I haven't mentioned how many laps I did or how far I ran and I'm not going to. Let's face it, that information is easily available if you really want to know. But this wasn't about that. This race really did transcend individual performance. It was all about the collective, all about the common goal to succeed. Maybe, after all these years, that is the real lesson from my journey. It's not about the personal bests and the medals, it's about the people we encounter along the way who make a difference to our lives. It's about the countless volunteers I've encountered, the race organisers, the announcer at the Brighton 10k, my friend Dan and the man who shouted to me at the London Marathon, "You've got this, Ash!" It's the pacemakers who've helped me to individual glory, the runner who said to me at the CCC, "Keep going." These and so many other people have touched my life and helped me become the runner I wanted to be. They are the real heroes of this journey, and when I think about running, they will forever be uppermost in my thoughts.

CHAPTER 24

FINAL THOUGHTS

I dread this session with a passion, more than any other part of my weekly training cycle. It's Wednesday evening, and the next hour has been on my mind since Monday. You see, running fast is not my thing; I'm content plodding along in my comfort zone. Speed takes me way outside that, and I don't like it – not one bit!

I've already covered two miles as a warm-up, and I'm about to start the first of my eight half-mile reps. Before beginning this venture into hell, I turn on my running playlist, consisting of songs that fire me up. The first track is a live version of Iron Maiden's ode to World War Two Spitfire pilots called "Aces High." Recorded in 1985, it's loud, brash, and bombastic, but most importantly, the song includes an excerpt from Sir Winston Churchill's rousing post-Dunkirk speech in 1940. You've probably heard it – it's the one that includes the heroic and inspiring words, "We shall go on to the end, we shall fight in France", and so on. It concludes with the words "we shall never surrender", and at this moment, Iron Maiden breaks into the pulsating song. Suitably roused and motivated, it's time for me to go to work!

I'm running each half-mile rep in a time of 2 minutes 55 seconds, or 5:50 per mile, with a 90-second recovery. The first three or four are okay, but come the fifth, the required effort and exertion this session demands begin to take their toll. This pace is fast, and by the end of rep five, I'm breathing heavily. Just about recovered, it's time to start rep six. With approximately 200ft of the rep to go, I'm hanging on. The ninety-second recovery is starting to feel far shorter than it did during the previous reps, and starting rep seven, I still haven't recovered – not even close. My heart is racing as I set off, and my breathing is laboured. It takes all the effort I can muster to get up to speed, and this time, it's only ¼ mile before I start to struggle. Just about making it to the end of the rep, I feel battered, exhausted, and sick. My mind starts playing tricks on me, "I'm not capable of another rep, no point even starting." The ninety-second recovery has felt closer to thirty, and all too soon, it's time to press the button on my watch to start the final rep. This is killing me, and the half-mile rep now feels like three! Rounding a kink in the road, I spot the post box that signifies I'm nearing the end – the last big effort tonight. Initially, it motivates me, but all too quickly, it seems like the red box is not getting any closer. My legs are buckling, and the lactic build-up torturing my muscles makes me want to stop. "Dig deep, keep going, it's nearly over." With one final push, I run past the post box, and at last, it's all done. Hands on my knees, coughing and wheezing, the sweat is dripping off my face and body. I'm utterly shattered and dreading the prospect of the two-mile cooldown run back home.

Tomorrow, I have a five-mile easy run, followed by 7 miles at race pace on Friday. Saturday is 6 miles, easy, and on Sunday, I have 21 miles at an easy effort, with the last three of those miles at race pace. Monday brings the relief of a rest day before the whole process starts again on Tuesday with 6 miles of easy running.

Seems like a strange place to start a closing summary, don't you think? Well, this has been an average training week for me during the last seven or so years, and I'm beginning to feel it. The niggling injuries are starting to mount up, and mentally, it's becoming harder to raise my game, to keep pushing myself in those tough training sessions. I've also entered my fifties, and during this decade, things will begin to change, and maintaining my fitness will become ever harder. I can't cheat aging, and slowing down is inevitable. If I'm honest, that scares me a little. There is a part of me now that is ready to take it easier, to enjoy the views when I'm out running. To stop and smell the flowers and to take photos. But there is another part of me that still wants to compete. To strive to be the very best that I can be. Which side of me wins? Well, only time will tell. One thing I do know is, as I enter my 6th decade, running faster is going to get harder – if not impossible.

But that is okay, and what I can promise you is this. The last seven years have been an incredible journey, and I wouldn't have missed it for the world. From cityscapes to the beautiful rolling hills of the English countryside, to the majestic mountains of Wales and the Alps, I've seen nature at its beautiful best. I have achieved more than I ever thought possible, and looking back now, sometimes I can't believe that was me. Did I really do all that? It's beginning to feel like a distant memory already. I guess one of the big questions would be, did I really reach my full potential? Well, I suppose that is the six million dollar question to which we may never know the answer. I'd like to think that in the end, I got fairly close. Perhaps my biggest victory is running past that house from my childhood. A place that holds haunting memories that still leave me scarred to this day. When I was a young boy, I just wanted to run away from there and never look back. I'm not sure whether or not running towards my past really made any difference in the end, but at least I know I'm no longer running away. I'm in danger of writing my own eulogy here, and if I sound a little mawkish, I don't mean to be. Every journey has to come to an end, but just as one journey concludes, a new one begins. It's just that the route and the destination might be different. That sounds very exciting to me. There are new places to run, new experiences to be had, and new people to meet, and I can't wait!

Lastly, my big hope in sharing my story is this: I aspire to inspire you to embark on your own journey of discovery, to find your personal crossroads, and to choose the path marked – What if? I envision someone putting down this book, donning a pair of running shoes, and stepping out the door to commence their adventure. If you've ever pondered what could happen if you truly tried, I say go for it – scratch that itch! Venture out there and run faster, further, or higher than you ever have before. Explore new places and embark on new adventures. You are never too old, too young, or too unfit to attempt it. It takes courage, determination, patience, and a lot of hard miles. But more than anything else, it takes belief – belief in yourself. If you learn to believe and trust in the power within you, you might just be surprised by what you are capable of. But whatever running means to you – whether it's speed, distance, or something else entirely – our reasons for running are unique to us, after all. As long as it brings a smile to your face, makes you happy, and gives you that warm sense of achievement, that is all that matters.

And what about my future? Well, who knows? Currently, I'm relishing the opportunity to spend more time with my beautiful wife, Jane. After all she's done for me, I believe I owe her that. Perhaps one day, I'd like to try my hand at a triathlon – though that does mean learning to swim! Or maybe I'll revisit the 100-mile Grand Slam – who knows? It could be that I run the North Downs Way 50. After all, I've never actually raced it properly, have I? And who knows, I might even open a Strava account! One thing I do know for certain is that I love to run, and I can't imagine my life without it. Whatever I'm doing, wherever I am, I know I'll still be pounding the streets and the trails, churning out the miles. And the best thing of all? Never again will I find myself wondering… what if?

CHAPTER 25

ERNIE AND JUNE

I couldn't possibly conclude this book without introducing you to two very special people who collectively had a profound and lasting impact on my life. Ernie and June are my grandparents, and amid a turbulent and troubled upbringing, they provided me with warmth, love, and the opportunity to experience childhood like a proper little boy.

Ernie and June, my father's parents, resided in Bexhill-on-Sea in East Sussex. I would spend the entire school summer holidays with them, and those blissful, seemingly endless sunny days are the happiest memories I have from my childhood. My grandparents were not wealthy, and they both worked hard to pay the mortgage on the council house they had bought. I vividly remember accompanying my Grandad to work, either in a home for adults with learning difficulties or in the newsagents, where I would sit next to him while he served his customers. I recall the lovely parrot in the shop that would greet customers with a squawk or even a word. When Grandad wasn't working, we would walk for hours in the countryside, me by his side, holding his strong hand, looking up at this gentle giant of a man. Often, I would wear a hat my Grandfather had made for me out of old newspapers. Inevitably, we would end up at a pub where Grandad would have a pint while I tucked into crisps and squash before we made our happy way home, through fields and woods or sometimes along the seafront promenade. We would chat for hours as we meandered along, basking in the warm summer sunshine. If I wasn't with Ern, I would be with my Nan at one of her cleaning jobs. After work, we would find somewhere to kick a ball around. Even though she would've been tired after a hard morning at work, she always had time for a game of football. Or, if not football, we would go swimming at the local lido, and if I were lucky, we'd pick up a fish & chip supper on the way home! Nan bought me my first cricket bat, nothing special or expensive, but I loved that bat and played with it for hours until it finally broke. My wonderful Nan and Grandad always had time for me. We would eat together and discuss our daily plans at breakfast, and over dinner, we'd talk about what we'd been up to during the day. They would sit for hours, watching my hopeless magic shows, desperately trying not to laugh as every trick went wrong, while clapping and offering endless encouragement. At bedtime, they would read me stories and tuck me in for the night, and there were always more hugs than one boy could ever cope with! How I wished those summer holidays would last forever.

Grandad had served with the Royal Navy during the Second World War. In 1942, he was sailing aboard HMS Sikh when it was part of the flotilla that chased down and sunk the mighty German ship – Bismarck. My Dad tells a wonderful story of a cinema trip with Grandad to see the film "Sink the Bismarck!" Since HMS Sikh had been part of the flotilla that chased her down, Grandad got free tickets to see the film! HMS Sikh took part in a Commando raid named Operation Agreement off Tobruk, Libya, in September 1942. During the mission, she came under heavy fire, resulting in her being sunk with the loss of nearly 120 seamen. Grandad survived and spent six months as a prisoner of war before being repatriated back to England. Upon his return, he resumed active duty with the Royal Navy, rising to the rank of Leading Seaman and at times, an acting Petty Officer, before retiring in 1955. He served on a ship called

HMS Duncan at one stage of his career. It gives me great pride to tell you that Duncan is mine and my father's middle name. I'd known since I was little that Ernie had served with the Royal Navy, but it wasn't until recently that I managed to discover his records and the full extent of his career. His service record and replicas of his campaign medals hang proudly on a wall in my home. One of millions of war heroes to the nation, to me, he was the best, most gentle grandfather a little boy could ever wish for. Sadly, he passed away in 1983 when I was just 10 years old, and I still miss him to this day. But by then, he had deeply inspired me, and the effects of that inspiration remain to this day. I aspire to be the man my grandfather was, and I hope I make him proud. I'm happy and thrilled to report that my wonderful Nan, who now lives in Battle, East Sussex, is going strong to this day. And long may that continue!

My grandparents never spoiled me. Instead, they offered me tenderness, attention, affection, and love. They were a shining beacon of light during dark days, and I have no idea what would have become of me without them. Their actions taught me what it was to be considerate towards other people, the importance of simple acts of kindness, to listen to others, and to take pleasure in the simple things in life. If there is any good in me now, I owe that to my Nan and Grandad, and I will be forever grateful for their love and guidance. This book is dedicated to them both, and I love them with all my heart. Now, I wonder if Nan fancies a kickabout!?

ACKNOWLEDGEMENTS

I'd like to take a moment to thank the following people.

My amazing wife, Jane Varley. Without her endless love, patience and unwavering support, none of this would've been possible. I love you, sweetheart.

My Dad, Peter Graves. For being my number one fan! Love you.

My Auntie Sue, for always listening and encouraging me to publish this book. I love you, dearest aunt.

My Nan and Grandad, (June & Ernie) for giving me a childhood. As the song goes - God only knows what I'd be without you. Love always.

Paul McCleery, Danny Blackman & Lucy Martlew. Three of the greatest companions a man could ever have on a long run. Love you, guys.

Yanina Goldenberg and her team for helping me to edit and publish this book.

Emma Stubbs and Andy Lee for being the first to read and review my story.

Everyone at Hastings Runners for showing me the way in the early years.

My physio, Kimberley Kempster, for keeping injury at bay.

All of the race directors, pacemakers, my fellow runners and the countless volunteers who have been part of this story. Thank you for being there guys. You are amazing.

And, last but not least. Anyone else I may have forgotten! Thank you too, I couldn't have done it without you.

Printed in Great Britain
by Amazon